False Accusations

False Accusations

By Nik Greene

Strategic Book Group
Durham, Connecticut

Strategic Book Group
P. O. Box 333
Durham, CT 06422
http://www.strategicbookclub.com

ISBN: 978-1-60976-056-4

Book Design by Julius Kiskis

Printed in the United States of America
19 18 17 16 15 14 13 12 11   1 2 3 4 5

Dedication

To dedicate this book to one person would be a betrayal.

To those who helped me to weather the storm, I thank
you from the bottom of my heart.

To those of you who created it, I thank you from the heart
of my bottom.

Acknowledgements

To my wife, Trudy: Thank you for sitting through the clenched teeth, the quiet moods, and the tears, and for mopping my brow during the nightmares and pretending it didn't hurt you.

To my son, Tyler: Thank you for your support and for understanding that Dads are not always invincible.

Evelyne: Thank you for not just speaking my words.

John MR: Thank you for your energy, your humor, and your strength. Shukufuku-shin.

Gordon & Denise: Thank you for going the extra mile.

To all my friends I am not naming: You all know who you are, and I am worried I might miss one out. Your support was what kept me going and still does to this day.

To the doubters and those who went out of their way to make things worse: If even once it pricks your conscience, that's enough for me.

CHAPTER ONE

The Whys and Wherefores

Knowing where to begin is easier said than done. Starting from the beginning is all very well, but where is the beginning? To my way of thinking, the beginnings can be endless, depending on your viewpoint of the subject, but I digress. My thoughts and words are not here to change your (the reader's) life, but are for me a way to exorcise my demons. I am attempting to put down the words that I haven't been able to speak. I desperately want to be able to move on, to come to terms with a life I never thought I would experience firsthand.

I still, to this day, have not come to remember, apart from in the nightmares, every detail of what went on. And some of what I do remember, I cannot put into words. How do you word that kind of "despair" or "fear" so that someone will understand exactly what you went through?

I don't want just to put down inane facts. I want to try and get over my thoughts and emotions, as well as my thought processes, chronologically. Writing this way, I think you will understand a bit about the way I dealt with things and the way I controlled my emotions, as they all have a bearing on each other. As you read, I want you to try to "feel" too. In the end, this whole story is just about feelings. I want you to feel my confused loyalty for two children I grew to love as my own, as well as the same two children I am now supposed to despise.

Why am I writing this? I am writing this primarily because I have to, for my own benefit. But I am also writing this because I want others to know what it is like to have a dream destroyed – maybe not just a dream, but your every wish destroyed, everything you ever did or questioned, every good you put out into the world turned around for bad.

The story may seem a little one-sided, as it is heading toward a goal of writing my thoughts on a particular incident, but that's because it isn't a history of us. I will, however, give you an outline of our lives and the reasons behind our actions to give you some kind of framework.

CHAPTER TWO

The Beginnings

I had considered using a pseudonym when writing this book, but decided it would be more honest not to do so. I have chosen, however, not to reveal the real names of the people directly involved.

I met my first wife in 1981 and married her in 1984. We had a son in 1990, but divorced in 1992.

I love children and love being around them. I seem to have an affinity for making them smile, even when they are crying. I would have liked to have had more. I always used to say that I would like a minimum of two, but it wasn't to be.

The divorce from my first wife was traumatic, but I made it clear from Day One that I would not be a "two hours on a Sunday afternoon" type of dad. Luckily, although there was some animosity between me and my first wife, we actually made sure together that I never lost my son due to a divorce, like so many others. It was hard at times, more so because the wife from whom I had broken away was still "calling the shots." But, of course, the upshot of it all was that I got what I wanted. I had my son with me every moment I could, from Friday nights to Monday mornings, when I would drop him back off at school, and on most school holidays, too.

My ex-wife was going through a bit of a "finding herself crisis," so I had the benefit of that also, inasmuch as our son, Tyler, was often "in the way" for her.

We made it through together and, even now as a young man, he recalls the times with much happiness. It still brings me joy to hear him say, "Do you remember when, Dad . . . "

After a wild few years of being single again, I eventually met Trudy in 1994, and we married in 1995.

Trudy was not really the type of woman I had gone for previously, but falling in love again doesn't allow for type. She was strong and intelligent, yet vulnerable and kind. She was a strong-willed person with an ability to love very deeply. She could hurt very deeply, too, which is the downside.

If there was ever such a thing as a soul mate, she was mine.

Where Tyler was concerned, he was never introduced to any of my "acquaintances" unless I thought the relationship would go further. I eventually introduced him to Trudy about three months into the relationship. I would always have my weekend contacts with Tyler separate from those with Trudy, but I introduced them coming up to the Christmas holidays so Trudy and Tyler would have a good chance to get to know each other. They took to one another immediately, and she quickly became his "mummy two" (in his words, which he even uses now at the age of twenty).

Trudy had not had any children. While she had never expressed any interest in having any of her own, she, too, had a way with them. She loved being around the children of her friends and family members. I always said she would have made a great mother, as she had a maternal glint in her eyes.

Her brother was a foster caregiver and had fostered many youngsters. She had always helped, even to the point of being an "official" respite caregiver for her brother when he needed a break.

Long story short, we were approached about becoming foster caregivers by the local social services, as they were in dire need of caregivers at the time. We agreed and went through a vetting and training process taking almost two years. Our whole lives were analyzed for suitability.

The day came when we were approved by a panel of twelve people, so all we had to do was sit and wait for our first children or child to arrive. It was an exciting time for us. We actually felt as though we would be able to do something fantastic, worthy. This was the beginning of being able to give something back to society. It sounds corny, but we truly felt like that. Instead of just seeing TV advertisements depicting children in need, we were actually doing something to make a difference.

Regarding these early years of fostering, I am just going to glance over the history and bring to the fore points that will mean something later.

Two foster children, Naomi and David, joined our family in 1998. Naomi was six years old, and David was seven.

During the phone call from social services, we were told that nothing of any consequence was known about the family. We were advised to just see how things progressed, making sure that everything was documented. This, I must say point blank, was their first lie. These children and their six (at the time) other siblings had been on the "at risk" register since 1990. We didn't find this out until a good deal later.

Naomi and David turned up at the door escorted by

two social workers and their "nanny." They were scared out of their wits, but had quite a confident air about them – probably the result of a "fight or flight mechanism," but "an air" nonetheless.

Although they were only aged six and seven, you could see that they were small for their ages. Getting them onto scales later revealed that David weighed twenty-six pounds and Naomi weighed twenty-eight pounds – less than half of what their weights should have been. They were very gaunt and undernourished, and they both had very grey skin and sunken eyes. They brought tears to my eyes.

Naomi was tiny in stature, being just under a meter high with a little "bob" haircut. For all her frailty, she had a little, round face that broke into a nervous smile. Her green eyes didn't smile, though – just her mouth. She launched into a nervous diatribe about where she had come from and why she was here, then she started talking very quickly about the doll she was carrying in her left hand. A carrier bag in the other hand contained all her worldly goods, which consisted of nothing, really, but a dress and a pair of high-heeled shoes with a broken heel.

David was very quiet. He was also very gaunt with a basin-type haircut. All he was carrying was a pair of headphones with no lead attached. His blue eyes were almost invisible due to his fear-dilated pupils.

The clothes they stood up in, smelly and too small by far, were all they had.

Their first evening with us was made into a welcoming celebration. We had a family dinner of "party picky bits," as Trudy calls them. Immediately, we could see that the children had absolutely no idea how to sit at a table and eat, let alone use a knife and fork. All they knew how to eat was chips, biscuits, and chocolate – using their hands and stuffing the food into their mouths like it was their last meal for a week. They also put food in their pockets to take to bed with them. We later found out that they never knew when they would eat again, so when they received food, they hoarded it like squirrels. We also found that if they had to be disciplined verbally, they would find their way to the fridge and steal food because, as a punishment, their father or mother would refuse them food, sometimes for days on end.

They had absolutely no boundaries. No one had ever cared to give them any instruction on how to eat or wash, when to sleep or get up, how to speak properly, or even to ask for something. They were uneducated, having never really been registered in any school. They could only just basically read and write.

Over the coming weeks, we quickly learned about the children, hearing quite clearly about the abuses they had suffered at the hands of their natural parents. These abuses included violence and sexual abuse, and were even relayed in pretty clear and sometimes graphic detail. At the time, it hurt terribly to hear those kinds of things out of the mouths of such young children, awoke anger and emotion like no other; one of heartache for their suffering and anger that not just one person but a family could treat these children in such a way. We were taught, however, during our eighteen month fostering courses and evaluations to deal with this in an almost clinical manner, so as not to show the children involved that we were upset. This way, they would not feed off our emotions but would allow them to say what they had to say in their own ways. Then, we were to respond in an almost matter-of-fact manner, even thanking them for being "honest" with us, as was the normal response, and telling them they could tell us what they wanted, as this was their "safe family."

Every allegation and every story, however small, was documented in what turned out to be a day-to-day diary. Trudy and I would sit down after they had gone to bed and write down what had been said. Many times, we would actually cry together, too.

That day-to-day diary then turned into a large ring-binder file so that the pages could be easily removed to copy.

We would have a social worker come to the house probably two to three times a month to copy the documents and discuss what had been said. Occasionally, with something particularly poignant, we would call them at their offices and either have a meeting with them or they would come to us.

One sticking point was that social services only had "accommodation" rights. This meant that the birth family still had contact rights with Naomi and David, but it came to a point where we were feeling more protective of the children.

It was a struggle between their rights and what was right. We had to listen to the details of abuse on one hand, then take them to visitations with the father, mother, or nanny at their homes. It eventually came to a head, and I refused. I put my foot down and said to the worker at the time, "If you wish to put them in danger of continued abuse, you take them." There was no way that I, as their "safe parent," could deliver them into what I perceived as a lion's den every week.

After many meetings and many arguments, it was dealt with legally. All the evidence was presented, and it was eventually decided that "accommodated" would become "removed," so as to give the social services more say. It was also recommended that a police investigation commence to back up the ruling.

Officers came to our home to interview the children. Additionally, on a number of occasions, the children had to go to a special police house where whatever was discussed was recorded on video. We were not allowed access to this and sat in a waiting room while this went on, but we were told the details after each interview.

The rules were similar to the ways we were taught – no leading questions, no prompting, just natural progression. But in a calm, controlled, and recorded situation, this in itself caused a great deal of chagrin and frustration, not just with the police and fostering authorities, but also with us. As hard as the officials tried, the children stayed very guarded, never once saying anything remotely derogatory about their natural parents. I remember very well sitting and watching them "play" with the officers in the moments before the actual, official interview started, before the cameras were switched on to record. I can remember thinking at the time that they knew exactly what they were doing. Even at only seven and eight years old, they were not just aware of being controlled, but were aware of the cameras the whole time.

This course of action was eventually dropped with nothing achieved.

Hindsight is a marvelous thing. Looking back and considering what was to haunt us later, I would have done things a little differently, especially in regard to taking what both the children and social services were saying as gospel. Not being able to question the children further for fear it might "lead them," or, when we raised a question to Social services, have a hand waved at us in dismissal.

We were, I think, being dragged along not just by a process, but by a process with an ulterior motive – not to help the children but to get a safe conviction, to cover their own asses and justify a budget increase because of extra expenditure.

Don't get me wrong – at the time, we, too, were blinded by what we thought would lead to justice for these children and by the drama made of it all by social services.

As we were told so many times, "How could one child be so clear and precise with such detail if it wasn't true?"

That one sentence alone came back to bite us in the rear – hard. If I thought it would fit on the front cover, I would use it as this book's title.

As time progressed, social services got want they wanted. They had full control of the whole family, including siblings that were born in the years after. The mother gave birth to two more children, and immediately they were removed for adoption. In fact, adoptive parents were found before the birth. A "nanny" looked after two other siblings under social service care orders, and other siblings were either adopted or fostered out.

For our two, things started to settle down, and the children progressed slowly with their obvious problems – David with his autism and Naomi with her lying, deceit, and general behavioral problems.

Naomi also progressed with her verbal and mental control over David. It was a very strong kind of hold, forcing David to do anything she said without another thought. In life, there are always "leaders and followers," but some stand out among others, becoming famous or even infamous. David Koresh and other guru-type leaders who cast spells over other humans come to mind. But, to me, for a little girl of age eight to do this is unreal, and I would probably question anyone else who said it if I had not seen it with my own eyes.

One particular instance of "collusion" comes to mind, as it wreaked havoc on the family for a couple of weeks.

Naomi and David were visiting their nanny. Occasionally, the children's social worker, Alice, would "pop in" to make sure everything was going smoothly.

Now, Alice was not long out of college and in her mid-twenties. She was pretty with dark, copper-colored hair and was very, very loud. She would bound into a room and send everyone flying with her words. She reminded me of "Tigger" in the Winnie-the-Pooh stories.

This is all very well if you don't mind boisterous personalities, but it played havoc with the children, who, as you can imagine, were easily roused into boisterousness themselves.

On this particular occasion, Alice had probably wound the children up into a frenzy. Naomi started acting up, and Alice said to her, "If you don't start behaving, I will tell your foster parents when I take you home."

Naomi responded, "You cannot do that because they will hit me with a wooden spoon, won't they David?" David replied in the affirmative. In her blustery way, Alice reported this straight to social services, thus starting an investigation into whether we "hit" the children. In the end, after a lot of questioning all round, David admitted to one of the workers that it wasn't true. He explained that he had affirmed the "hitting" because Naomi had made the claim, and he was frightened of what she might say if he disagreed with her.

I can remember telling Tyler that my stepfather used to smack us with a wooden spoon. He would even put it in his bag or my mother's handbag and take it with him in case we misbehaved. All I can imagine is that Tyler either told this to Naomi, or she overheard a conversation about this and latched onto it.

Naomi never took the words back, but when asked questions by investigating workers, she just refused to answer them or changed her story.

This wasn't the first time Naomi had tried this in the family, but it was the most serious due to the aftermath. Naomi never spoke to us about it again, even much later when we asked her why she did such a thing to people who cared about her. She would put on a face of indignation fit for an adult, shrug her shoulders, and flit off to something else.

A particularly poignant issue to raise, as it comes out later, is that over the next couple of years we were asked a number of times by social services if Naomi would be willing to have an "examination" to verify sexual abuse. This would allow her to possibly bring charges against her parents "should she choose to" at a later date. We left the decision to Naomi and, although adamant at first that she did not want this, she eventually agreed. We and social services made her understand that this may be a good idea should she at some time want to bring charges and get some kind of "closure."

It was all arranged by the social worker, and all we had to do was to show up on the scheduled day.

The actual day it happened was quite harrowing for all concerned. I had to take Naomi to the examination, as Trudy was working and could not get the time off. Being the male, I was a little uneasy about this, but Naomi was fine with it and asked for me to stay with her even in the consulting room, and the nurses agreed. Naomi had lulled even me into a false sense of security with her. I thought for many years that we had a good relationship. Considering that it had been the "males" in her life that had done her the most harm, I was flattered that she considered me worthy, even though I was the male party.

The image from that day of Naomi with her legs trussed up in a harness while they hastily went about their business doing an internal examination using metal implements has stayed with me to this day. What got to me the most was Naomi's face as she turned and looked at me with a tear running down her cheek and absolute sorrow on her face.

I have never seen, before or since, such true, real emotion from her.

I had a quiet word with the nurses afterward, and they told me there was indeed some damage. The exam indicated that she had no hymen and that there was some scarring to the vagina wall, but the nurses said that this would by no means have any effect on her in later life in regard to having a child, etc.

Naomi was a very brave girl being subjected to this, and we took her out for a treat afterward to take her mind off the subject. She actually never spoke of it again.

We received a letter a couple of weeks later saying basically what the nurses said to me. Naomi was also given a copy of the letter to open when she was older, and the age of sixteen was hinted at. We have the letter to this day. A copy went to social services, and how to proceed was discussed at a meeting. Although some saw this as confirmation of abuse, others – including, oddly enough, the person who suggested the course of action – said it was not enough evidence to proceed and that, out of concern for Naomi's dignity, it should be left for her to decide in her own time what to do about it.

Over time, their lives changed for the better. Their schooling was vastly improved and, where David was concerned, he was getting the extra help.

Naomi became so blasé about the abuses that, early on, she would just mention it to anyone – even a surprised checkout girl in a local supermarket.

"Hello, my name is Naomi and these are my new parents, because my real parents were bad. . . . "

We, of course, added that to her "boundaries list."

CHAPTER THREE

Permanency and Adoption

I n about 2001, social services asked us if we would like to go for "permanency." While the children were already settled into our family, we were "officially" only classified as "short-term foster caregivers." So we would have to go through a minor vetting process, but this was academic.

We agreed that it would be good for the children and would give them extra stability in their lives to know that they would no longer be "farmed off" to another family if something happened. The children thought this was great, too, as to them it added security.

Then again, after another year or so, we were asked whether we would like to "adopt" them. Initially, we said no because of the "birth family" being so close. But with a bit of persuasion, we eventually agreed and the process began.

Although the adoption process went off without a hitch, it was a very lengthy process, taking a good six months or so. The courts assigned a psychologist to interview everyone independently, from the original family to us. He also interviewed both Naomi and David, and found that, psychologically, the children were happy with the adoption. But he did also lay out a few "caveats" concerning growing up with the "abuse" and how they would deal with it.

One thing I want to add at this juncture is that, when the psychologist asked about the abuse from their family members, the children wouldn't say anything. They would just ignore the questions, very similarly to the way they would "avoid" the subject when at the police house. At the time, this troubled us. But we, like everyone else, just put it down to the trauma of it all, believing that they were not ready to talk openly but happy to talk to us as their "safe family." The psychologist did say that, even with all their experiences of abuse, the children didn't behave in a manner similar to other abused children of the same age. He went on to say on record that not all children are the same, and that they do not all fit the scenarios expected of them.

The adoption went ahead, and all was well. It was almost like the children breathed a sigh of relief. We did also, because to some extent having social services around all the time was a strain in itself. And from the moment the children were adopted, they seemed to drop us like hot potatoes, obviously taking the line that they were already very busy and didn't need to bother themselves with us anymore.

This is something that, in hindsight, I think should be addressed. This is especially the case as, when my wife contacted the adoption agency for assistance with the case, they basically left us out to dry. It's not their concern, apparently.

Things once again settled down to some normality after a big party.

We had already talked about finding a "holiday home in France," but it progressed to a full-time home.

So, in this year, about six months after the adoption, we managed to sell our property in the UK, pool our resources, and just leave to start a new life in a new country. We obviously asked permission from the adoption agency, even though it wasn't really necessary.

The move was the right one, and this was the only time we could have achieved it without too much disruption to schooling, etc.

Naomi was at the age when she would enter senior school. Tyler was about to choose options. And, where David was concerned with his special needs, it didn't really matter as long as we could get him into an appropriate school to be able to deal with his disabilities in France where he could make some progress. I always believed that he had more in him, and I believed the school he was in "kept him down."

As a very brief example, one day, at the age of twelve, he came home waving a certificate around. So as not to disappoint him, we showed how happy we were for the achievement. But, at the time, I was not overly impressed that it was an A+ certificate achieved simply for successfully "drawing around his hand." He could do better than that, and we could get more from him personally than that. David, being David, would only give what he knew the person expected from him.

Everyone was very excited. Trudy, as his mother, had a few misgivings about David missing his friends as well, but these were soon sorted out and everything was ready.

We began a new life that represented a fresh start for everyone.

Chapter FOUR

France

I am not going to go on about the reasons we left the UK. They were many and varied, but it suffices to say that it was a decision we all made for the good of all. Not one of us pressured another. As a family, we all had an input, as was the way with our family always. We were and still are a "talking family." If a question was raised, we dealt with it. We didn't lie, embellish, or subdue a subject for any reason, whether it be Father Christmas or sex. The latter, especially, was dealt with in a formal but appropriate manner. We thought this especially important due to the abuse the children had suffered in their past.

As it was such an issue in their past, we didn't want them to think that it would remain so. It wasn't wrong and it wasn't dirty. At the right time and in the right way, it was a beautiful thing.

One good reason for leaving the UK behind was what I always called "getting back to basics." I was raised on a farm from a very young age. It was real, and I knew what it was like to work hard to produce something, whether it is a vegetable or an animal for food.

Children today live in this little cocooned life, not

allowed to get hurt, make mistakes, or compete in case they lose, mollycoddled by a nanny state. With the way our kids were raised in their formative years, I wanted to show them there was a real life out there, and France was the place to do it.

Another reason was the children's propensity to follow "charismatic" children, usually those who could get them into trouble.

France again offered a very different way with children. They are respected as a part of the family, and they, in turn, respect their family. It's a different culture and something we could all benefit from.

Time passed and everyone settled into a life in France, progressing really well with a lifestyle change as well as a new language.

We lived in the barn in two separate caravans. We had a more private area for Naomi, being the only girl among two boys, until we got the bedrooms done so they could move in. My first priority was to finish the first floor so that the kids could all have back their own space and so that, in time, all the children could enter puberty in a little more privacy.

Thinking their past would catch up with them as their bodies changed and hormones raged, we expected this to be a harrowing time for Naomi and David. But we were pleasantly surprised as to how well they were handling it. Our "talking family" had its fair share of discussions, but overall was progressing with dignity.

At this time, my own son announced that he was "gay." It caused a bit of disharmony between David and Tyler. And, to be honest, it caused some troubles for me also. I have never seen being gay as anything other than a perversion, and to this day still have a problem with it in the back of my mind. I, like many, I presume, learned to live with it, as it is an accepted norm in this day and age. I just had to adjust my way of thinking about my own son. After all, my son is my son, and being gay doesn't change anything on a family level. I wanted my son to grow up, get married, and have children – my grandchildren. But I see now that is my view of life and not his. Everything else about him I could not be more proud of.

David's problem with it was more about peer pressure. But as they grew up, that became less important, largely because they didn't spend an awful lot of time together as they went to different schools, and then Tyler went on to *lycée.*

As far as Naomi was concerned, she grew up and got louder and more boisterous. But, as a daughter, she was very loving and caring, though in a very shallow, immediate kind of way. If we had been apart for some reason, when I walked in the door she would yell, "Daddy Pumpkins" and throw herself at me. She would always be around to help with the various building projects, but would also tend to flit about a bit. She was called more than once by the French term "papillon," or butterfly in English.

As far as puberty went, she never really grew up. She changed physically and started her menstrual cycle, but mentally she never changed. It became a bit of a problem at times, as she would do things without thinking – like cartwheels in the garden while wearing a skirt and flimsy top with no bra, so that everything would be on show, very often with visitors around. Unless prompted, she would not behave with dignity during her period, at times having blood on her garments.

On the other hand, her propensity for talking to the boys in a sexual manner and boasting to her friends about her sexual experiences with her previous family became a problem. On a number of occasions, we were called to the school or sent letters asking if we would do something about her "flirtatious" behavior.

It became a bit of a "nagging point" from both myself and Trudy, with many discussions held about how she should be more aware of the fact that she was changing and could not behave like a young girl any longer. Apart from sitting her down and talking it through with her about the reasons and dangers, we were just weathering the storm, hoping it would eventually settle down as she grew up. We thought it was just her way of dealing with the past.

How wrong could we have been? At the age of fourteen, Naomi's world changed, and all hell broke loose for us as a family.

In hindsight, somehow, I think that it had something to do with a "sleepover" with a friend of hers the weekend before. I don't know to this day whether her flirting got out of hand and a boy/man of twenty named Nicolas tried to take advantage, but she came home on the Sunday night a bit distressed. When asked what had happened, all she would say was, "He wouldn't leave me alone and kept talking in a sexual manner." She also had her period on that weekend and said Nicolas was embarrassing her about it.

She wouldn't let us pursue the matter, responding in her normal manner of changing the subject, but also saying it was fine.

CHAPTER FIVE
The Arrest

We found out some time later that Naomi had actually mentioned to a teacher on the Thursday of this week that I had abused her. Nothing was said by anyone, including Naomi. That following weekend, Naomi appeared to be behaving normally, showing absolutely no sign whatsoever of what she had done. She was her normal self, even on the Monday morning with her goodbye at the door going to school.

The first thing to happen was that I received a phone call requesting that I go to the *gendarmerie* (French police station) in the local town at 14:00, with no indication as to why. Both Trudy and I put it down to a dog we had found the week before. Maybe they wanted to know some details.

We had absolutely no idea of what was to come.

I walked through the door of the *gendarmerie*, not thinking for one moment I wouldn't be walking out of it very soon.

I introduced myself to the officer behind the desk. I had seen the man, a very short and dark-haired officer with very dark eyes topped by a monobrow, around the town. He always struck me as arrogant. At the same time, a guy by the name of Frankie introduced himself to me as the translator asked by the *gendarmes* to assist with the interview. It was at this point that I knew something a bit more serious than a dog was the issue. I remember my mind racing at this point, wondering what it was I could have been called for. My immediate thoughts were that one of the kids had been in trouble. I was taken to a room that looked like an office with two chairs in front of a desk.

One officer was behind the desk typing at a computer. He had a shaved head and was dressed in full *gendarme* blues broken only by gold jewelry. He wore big rings, a rope chain necklace, and a bracelet that clanked as he carried on typing. He looked at me and pointed to the chair to sit down. He unclipped his gun holster and put it on the desk in front of him. Whether this was a "don't mess with me" sign or the gun was simply uncomfortable on his hip, I don't know.

The monobrow officer who was at the front desk followed behind, joined by a third officer and Frankie. The monobrow officer sat at the end of the desk, and the third officer stood behind me. I remember his presence but not what he looked like at this point.

Frankie sat next to me, looking as nervous as I did.

Frankie reminded me of Jimmy Somerville from the band The Communards. He was just as gay, I thought at the time, and quite effeminate.

The gold-clad officer behind the desk looked up at me and stared for what felt like minutes, but was probably only a few seconds.

The *gendarme* then said the words, "Do you have any idea why you have been called here today?" At this point, my heart filled with anguish. The sound of one's heart and that feeling of a knot developing in the sternum is a feeling I never got used to as things developed over the next few days. Even writing this brings back that same feeling.

I answered, "No, not at all." He then continued almost as though he hadn't listened to what I had said, or had expected my answer.

"Your daughter has told us that you have been abusing her sexually over the last four years," he said. My first response was to laugh in a muted sort of way.

In a split second, thoughts, words, and sentences pass through one's head. But, for the life of me, I cannot recall them to put them down on paper. It suffices to say that fear washed over me in an instant. It felt like warm water starting from my head and face. I probably visibly blanched at his words. But apart from responding, "That's ridiculous," I was stunned into silence. The world around me sounded like a muffled tape player on half speed. The only time I felt anything similar was when, at the age of about fifteen, I saved my brother from drowning but nearly drowned myself in the process. I was drowning in emotion this time, not water.

It was something that we as a family had half expected, purely because we were told during our fostering courses that it could happen. And, during the period over which we had been looking after these foster children, we had been warned by a psychiatrist and the like that allegations of abuse were common. But words cannot describe adequately that feeling of hearing those words.

It's all very well, too, writing these words in English. But you have to remember that the *gendarmes* did not speak at all in English, so everything was said via the translator. Although, by this point, I could speak and understand

French quite well, so I was "picking up the tone" and the gist of the sentence before Frankie translated it. But I still waited for him to finish his translation.

I still think to this day that this situation hindered the case greatly. Everything I said had to be said twice, and I believe this delivers one's words out of context. For a start, the translator, as we found out later, was not very good. But the issue was predominantly that one cannot freely express one's feelings through mere words. Expression, sound, and body language are just as important, if not more so. Think of the words, "I love you." We can all say the words, but they only mean something with meaning and sincerity behind the voice of the speaker. Now imagine you want to say "I love you" to someone, but by using someone else to say it for you. Now think of "I did not do such a thing," and telling someone else to say your words for you!

Monsieur Jewelry or another officer typed each question asked into the computer as it was asked, then again as Frankie translated it. Apparently, Frankie was not translating very well, either, as he had to keep repeating my answers as the officer was typing. Monsieur Jewelry had been brought in from 'Headquarters' in Limoges, which is probably the equivalent to the UK's Criminal Investigations Department (CID), and I think he had been watching too many bad cop movies. At times, he was very soft-spoken, speaking almost in a caring manner. Then, the next minute, he was very aggressive, banging the table and accusing me of being a pervert.

Sometimes he would sit behind the desk, typing his questions and my words. And, at other times, he would sit on the desk in front of me, trying to intimidate me by being in my space.

This aside, the questioning was serious and often very

personal due to the nature of the accusation. But it also ran long into the evening, as I was over and over again being asked the same questions. At about 5:00 p.m., I was told that we would be going to my home and that I had to sign a search order. I did so.

They handcuffed me with my hands at the front, and I was taken to a waiting car and driven to my house.

Two other vehicles followed with two officers in each, as there's nothing like a show of force for everyone to see.

I was told to stand in the kitchen with Trudy, but an officer kept us apart and we were not allowed to speak to each other.

They started in the lounge, going through all the books, cupboards, and boxes of photos and music discs. In some of the boxes, they found computer discs that they put into a supermarket shopping bag.

Then they moved upstairs to search the bedrooms individually. They took Tyler's laptop, Naomi's laptop, and photos and diaries from Naomi's room. They then moved on to our bedroom.

They went through everything and took anything they thought relevant, including a box of chocolates from a drawer. Every book on every shelf was searched. I had a built-in "office area" in the corner of the room, and this was ransacked thoroughly. Again, anything they thought relevant was put into shopping bags (that belonged to us) and removed.

I was bundled back into the car and taken back to the *gendarmerie.* and back into that little office.

Monsieur jewellery had carried the carrier bag in with him and put it on the desk in front of him. He stared at me a few seconds, rested on his knuckles on the desk top while leaning forward and said

"Was there anything in what they had collected that might incriminate me?"

"No, certainly not," I replied without a thought.

They had collected 3 computers.

"Was there anything on the computers that might incriminate me?"

"No, certainly not," again I replied

"Why were there chocolates in the cupboard drawer?"

This question threw me at first, "Errrr, we like chocolates?" I replied sarcastically

Monsieur Gold replied with, "Naomi said you bribed her with chocolates for sex," and waited for an answer as though it was a question.

I laughed at the statement. "Rubbish," I said

The questioning continued as such for another two hours.

At the end of this and every other session of questioning, which usually lasted about three or four hours at a time, the transcripts were printed out to be read over and confirmed as correct with a signature from each person in the room.

This first session ended at about 8:00 p.m., and I was sent to a cell. This was a horrid, grey-painted box about three meters square with a stainless toilet on the left and 2-inch rubber-foam mattress on a bed that was formed of concrete like the floor.

I sat down utterly exhausted and drained.

They went and had dinner.

Although Trudy had been told to go home earlier in the afternoon, she was told to come back later, as they wanted to question her and the boys. Luckily, she brought a sandwich with her and insisted that they give it to me. She also insisted that she be allowed to see me, and eventually was given permission to do so, but only for two minutes. I told her not to worry, that I would be home soon. At this point, I believed that this would be the case. But worry was setting in, as I knew they wouldn't allow me and Naomi to be in the same place at the same time.

That was the last time I saw Trudy and the rest of the family for a very long time.

After the officers had eaten, I was escorted back to the "office" at about 9:00 p.m. and questioned further. I was allowed to eat my sandwich in front of them, but it stuck in my throat like a golf ball, and I could only manage half of it.

I was eventually allowed to retreat to a cell at about 11:00 p.m., after a very tiring evening of being questioned over and over again.

I didn't sleep. Most of what was going through my head was – "Why?" Why would she do it? I was convinced that she must have said something stupid – maybe boasting or trying to impress – and it got out of hand.

I just lay on my back, staring at grey walls and imagining the answers for myself.

That chocolate issue got to me, too. The chocolates in the drawer were rather expensive ones that Trudy liked, and once in a while I gave the kids one as a treat with a "Don't tell Trudy" quip. But never did I think it would come back to bite me – never. It was simply an act of "Dad-style kindness."

I could hear noises above this grey cell. The *gendarmes* on duty obviously slept over or lived on the premises, and every couple of hours one of the bleary-eyed officers would come down to the cell, open the door, check on me, and close it again. I don't remember sleeping at all in the time I was there.

At about 7:00 a.m., I could again hear activity in the offices, but most officers returned at about 8:00 a.m. From then onward, the smells of breakfast cooking wafted through to the cell. And then, at about 9:00 a.m. or so on Day Two, my door was unlocked and I was demanded to leave the cell for another four hours of questioning.

I sat down and waited for Frankie to turn up. I was informed that he would be late, as he had a signing to do, but that he would be in time for the meeting with the judge in Limoges. I was informed that, on this day at about 3:00 p.m., I would be taken to Limoges to see a judge who, on the basis of what had been learned thus far, would make a decision on whether to allow another twenty-four hours of interrogation. I was told before this that it would be granted, and that the decision was just a legal formality.

I could either proceed without him or go back to the cell. I decided to proceed, albeit in French.

I decided to ask for a glass of water, as I certainly would not have been offered it. I was given a small bottle of mineral water, which was delivered with an indignant stare from the officer.

Questioning continued, in a slightly lighter way, about why we chose to adopt, etc. At about 12:30 p.m., I was sent back to the cell while the officers had dinner.

At 2:00 p.m., I was removed from the cell and taken back to the office. They explained what would happen at the court. By this time, Frankie had reappeared and was translating again for me.

At 2:30 p.m., I was handcuffed with hands in the front and loaded into a police van with another four officers and the translator. Another car carrying another three officers led the convoy. The journey seemed so long and surreal while handcuffed to the bodywork in the back of a *gendarme* vehicle. It wasn't the most comfortable ride to Limoges.

After we parked across the road from the court buildings, I was unceremoniously dragged, by the handcuffs and with everyone on the street looking at me, out of the vehicle, across the road, and up the steps into the main entrance hall. Being dragged by the handcuffs was, according to them, their way of safely transporting me through a public area and down to the cells under the court building. The cells, consisting of a tiled floor with cages instead of cubicles, looked like an underground public toilet, and smelled like one too.

I was unshackled and pushed into an open cage, which was covered in graffiti and only about two meters square. I was told that I would have to wait until the judge was ready to see me, which would be after she had read all of the information accumulated so far.

I waited for about an hour, sitting on hard, cold stainless-steel seating, when the door opened. I was then re-handcuffed and dragged to small room where two women sat at a table. One was a judge, and the other was a transcriber taking notes. The judge appeared to be in her fifties and had glasses perched on the end of her rather bulbous nose, causing her to look down her nose at the papers and up over the glasses at me. She stared at me for what seemed a minute or so, but in reality was probably just fifteen to twenty seconds. "Your name is Nicholas Simon Greene?" he asked in English. "Yes," I replied in English, but in a rather soft, dry voice.

She sharply said, "You must speak . . . stronger," meaning louder, of course. I coughed and answered again. She then proceeded to ask a number of basic questions pertaining to whether I understood the accusations and whether I was pleading guilty or not guilty. She asked all of her questions in English, apart from when the transcriber didn't understand something and she replied in French.

After having signed a few sheets of paper and passing them to me to sign, she said, "You are released to go." My heart skipped a beat, thinking for a split second that I could go home. But she must have seen something in my face and replied, "I am releasing you to the gendarmes, giving them further leave to question you for another twenty-four hours." As I got up, or, more accurately was hoisted up, she said to me in English, "I hope none of this is true." Before I had time to answer, I was yanked away and was back to being dragged through the court building. Personally, I feel this was very much uncalled for. No one else was treated in such a way, even though some were clearly there for a "hearing."

On the drive back to the *gendarmerie*, we took a detour to the local main police headquarters to drop off the laptops they had removed from my house. I sat handcuffed in the van with the doors wide open and only the translator for company. He didn't speak to me at all. In fact, by looking in the opposite direction, he made it obvious that he wasn't going to engage in conversation.

There was a bit of commotion when, as the gendarmes returned to the vehicle, they shouted at someone leaning out of the window. Even in French, I understood.

"Does he look like a English pervert?" the one on the inside asked.

"Come and have a look for yourself," the officer said.

Then Frankie looked at me to see if I understood.

As they got back into the van laughing, I said in English, "What does an English pervert look like then – any different to a French one?"

The question went unanswered, although the officer to whom I had spoken leaned over and undid my handcuffs.

Arriving back at the *gendarmerie* in my local town, I was walked out of the van to the back door. Even though the door was open, they congregated around it and got cigarettes out, offering me one, too. I refused, of course.

I just leaned up against the wall, waiting for them to finish puffing. I was then led back into the office for more questioning. I was still offered no food. I was only given my empty bottle of water back and told to "fill it up over there." I was again questioned until 11:00 p.m. and put back in the cell. I was told during this portion of questioning that the next step was to return to two different judges on the next day, and that the appointment had been made for 3:00 p.m. One judge was the *juge d'instruction* and the other was the *juge du detention*.

Questioning began the next day at 8:00 a.m. Again, I was offered no breakfast or lunch, just the same old questions.

This was the day when I was told that Naomi had been subjected to a medical examination. At first, my heart sank, remembering that first examination in a flash. Then, in that brief pause before they asked any more questions and awaited my response, panic set in. This was because, to my way of thinking, Naomi was no longer "a virgin" and, remembering the comments of the women at the first examination in the UK, was also scarred and damaged. My first thought was, "Oh my God, they are going to think it was me."

What came next shocked me to the core.

The lead investigator Monsieur Gold just said the word "negative" and, after a pause, "You look surprised."

Surprised was not the word. The last two days of questioning had been about the allegation that I had raped her – not just once, but "a number of times," including penetration.

He went on to say that the report was not just negative, but that her hymen was totally intact. Naomi was a virgin with no sign of damage in any way, whatsoever.

My immediate response to this was, "What am I still doing here?" My question again went unanswered.

They showed me the faxed report, which had been received that morning. I asked the translator to say, "Was this taken to the judge I had just seen?"

My question again went unanswered.

It was at this point that they put me back into the cell while they had lunch. But my mind started racing. Naomi had not only lied to the *gendarmes* and the teachers to instigate this inquiry. She had lied to us, to social services, and to her family in the UK from Day One. Then, what about the nurses who did the UK examination? How can two examinations be so clearly different? No, not just different, but completely opposite? Even though I didn't understand or have all the answers for myself, I had a ray of hope. It would be my "saving grace."

It also made nonsense of all the details I had given about her previous abuses. All of a sudden, *I* felt humiliated.

Who and what circumstances have contributed to the culmination of this accusation? Has Naomi been telling such a web of lies for so many years that she now no longer understands what is right and wrong? Alternatively, has it worked for her for so long that she has an ultimate reason for doing this?

Could social services and the doctors have conspired to get a result they wanted? And, if so, why?

Had Naomi and David just lied for the sake of lying? In one of the documented items, we remember Naomi saying that she and David sat and watched pornographic movies. Is this where they learned the ideas and terminology to lie so convincingly?

You have to understand – this is all "whizzing" through my mind like a whirlwind, and I'm still unable to make sense of any of it.

After lunch – their lunch, not mine – I was dragged back for more questioning.

The lead investigator leaned over me and said, with what seemed like sneering pride, "To answer your last question, 'Why am I still here?' – you are accused of rape, which, in France, includes oral sex, so nothing has changed."

To me, this seemed ludicrous.

Naomi had given explicit details about how I had raped her on one occasion, on a table, and it had now been proven a lie.

How could they go on believing that I had forced her into giving me oral sex? But they did.

They just ignored the fact that she was lying. The "negative" result didn't sway them in any way from their vehement questioning techniques.

After all, how could one child be so clear and precise with such detail if it wasn't true? She was a fourteen-year-old girl – she couldn't possibly lie about such a thing, now could she?

The time approached 2:00 p.m., and they had to prepare for a meeting with the other judges. They also told me that I would, at last, be able to see an *avocat* (a legal professional equal in rank to a magistrate or law professor). From this point, I will refer to him as "Maitre M," as this is his title.

Still without food of any sort since the half sandwich I managed to eat on Day One and feeling very weary, I was escorted away in the same manner as before, handcuffed and being pulled around like a slave in Roman times.

The first judge I was scheduled to see was the *juge d'instruction* (JI).

I was again dragged through the court building and down some stairs into the dungeon that was the holding cell. I was told to wait for Maitre M.

The role of an *avocat* in France is not the same as a lawyer in the UK. They are not really there to defend you, but to assist you. In fact, during the entire time I was being questioned, there were only a couple of instances when my avocat actually spoke to the JI. He is also there to make sure that laws are adhered to during the proceedings.

I was moved from the holding cell to a similar cell, this one with a small fixed table and two fixed chairs. Eventually, Maitre M turned up. He was tall for a Frenchman, a fairly good-looking man with dark, wavy hair and a friendly face and smile – which was not unwelcome at this juncture, I will say. He was wearing a black court gown and jeans. He had very deep, brown eyes, making him appear sympathetic, I suppose. I took to him right away. As he was let into the cell, he said in his best English, "Pleased to meet you, Mr. Greene." He explained who he was and described his position in the proceedings. He said, "I have read the dossier quickly, but would like you to tell me in your own words the reasons you are here." I started to do so.

Halfway through, he stopped me and asked me outright to tell him whether I was guilty or not.

"I am here to assist, whatever the case, but I need to know," he said.

I told him that I was absolutely not guilty of any of the accusations, and blurted on with the history behind the accusation as I saw it. I told him of my fears that I was not really being listened to, etc., and even said that Naomi's words were being taken as gospel without a thought.

He outlined the process and told me what to expect from each of the judges. He said that, even if things went badly and I was detained, he would get me out of prison within a day after finding somewhere I could go to stay, as Naomi was still at home. I gave options. His last words to me in the cell were, "She has been found as a liar, as her examination was negative. Everything will be okay." Famous last words indeed!

I met with the JI. She was a woman of about my age, maybe fifty, with blonde, greying hair, a slim build, and a very hard, pointed face, making her look very stern. She sat at an office table with another table ninety degrees to her left. There sat a friendly looking, dark-haired woman who smiled and nodded at me and took part in some friendly conversation with Maitre M. Eventually, she was introduced as the transcriber for the court.

The JI looked me up and down intently and launched into French chatter, which wasn't translated, so I presumed it to be legal requirements. She stopped abruptly, looked at me, and, with the opening statement, said something that in itself later led to a change in my translator and a great ally in the proceedings.

The JI started with, "You have been accused of raping and abusing your daughter. Did you do such a thing?"

My translator translated this as, "Do you understand that you are being accused of raping your daughter?"

I answered, "*Yes!*"

I only remember at this point Maitre M jumping in and saying something in French, but it wasn't until much later that I found out what was actually asked of me and to what I had admitted. I also find out later that this wasn't the last time a mistake was made during translation.

Then the questions continued in a similar vein to the police questions – same questions and answers, with me relying on the translator to repeat my and the JI's words accurately. I answered each question as clearly and concisely as possible, giving as much detail as I could about how I thought this could have happened. At the time, all I could answer was that the accusations had something to do with her past. Maybe memories from her past had jumped in time and she was accusing me of what her last family had done to her, I theorized. Maybe she had even said something stupid to her friends at school, and it had gotten out of hand.

After three days of questions, with no food and only water to drink, I was worn down. I really had no answers anymore. What more could I say? I didn't do what Naomi was accusing me of. How many times can you say you didn't do something? How many times can you come up with scenarios as to why she thought you did? I had no lies to tell, just thoughts. I had no stories to tell. All I could do was respond with the truth as I saw it.

I will say that the JI, although very stern, was not unkind in any way. She was vigorous in her speech but unbiased in her manner, clearly just seeking the facts.

In the room, the handcuffs were removed, but the group of six *gendarmes* sat on the floor behind me. When it was time to leave to go back to the holding cell and await the *juge du detention* (JD), I was again handcuffed.

Maitre M came to the cell and told me he thought it went okay.

The JD played exactly the role her name suggested. She

would decide whether I should be detained and for how long. But Maitre M didn't think I would be detained any longer than another day while they sought permission from the people I listed as potential hosts with places to stay.

It was now about 6:00 p.m., and I was very exhausted. I was again handcuffed and led down a corridor into a room that looked like a conference room for managerial staff. My handcuffs were removed as I entered, and I was led to the far end of the room, where I was told to sit down. Again, the *gendarmes* were all sitting behind me on the floor.

This judge was different. I noticed as I walked in the door and toward her that she did not take her eyes off of me, projecting an almost hateful stare. Even when I sat down, she kept her gaze fixed on me. I wasn't intimidated – I think I was too tired to be.

There were three others at the table – two transcribers, both women, and a rather official-looking man.

The JD's first words were, "You, monsieur, are a pervert, and I have the ability to put you in prison for twenty years." My *avocat* stepped in and spoke very quickly, by this time my mind didn't pick up the French but I presumed that he said something about the JD having no right to say this, but the words weren't translated.

I repeated that I was not guilty of these accusations and had never done anything remotely perverted in my life.

The JD then attempted to humiliate me by asking questions about my own sex life. Although I was embarrassed, I answered as clearly and concisely as possible without flinching. I don't generally like to discuss personal areas of my life with anyone, but after the last three days' events, my dignity was the least of my worries.

"How long have you been in France?" she asked. She

followed quickly with, "Why can't you speak French? Don't you think you should be able to speak French? Maybe prison will help you speak French."

I interrupted her spitting words with, "I do speak French, madam." I quickly added in my best French that I had a translator because I shouldn't be expected to deal with a legal situation in a second language in which I could not express myself as well.

I could not afford to make a mistake in my answers. She just "boffed."

"Boff" is a word the French use like the English "Huh!" – usually while tossing their head upward.

It shut her up for a second, though, especially as Maitre M cut in and defended me also.

After about half an hour of relentless questions, deliberation, and more questions, the JD announced without a second thought that she was going to send me to prison and that she would not even consider letting me out until she had received "favorable psychiatric reports."

The official-looking man to her right interjected in an undertone. Judging by the words I caught and his gestures, I thought he was protesting, but the JD wasn't to be moved. She had already made her mind up that I was guilty. I don't think she even listened to what I was saying or thought about what the written evidence had said. Maitre M seemed just as shocked as I was. He tried to apologize. He didn't understand why the JD was behaving in such a way, let alone how she came to the conclusion to send me to prison. At this point, my energy and spirit left me. I must have physically slumped, as Maitre M put his hand on my back and asked if I was okay. I was just stunned into silence by her obvious bigotry. Anyway, at this point, I was just too exhausted to do or feel anything else.

I was helped to my feet, once again handcuffed, and pulled out of the room.

This time, I was guided straight out the back door to the side entrance of the court building.

The *gendarmes* and Maitre M used this time to light cigarettes and chat about the case. I just leaned up against the wall, awaiting my fate. Maitre M turned to me and told me not to worry, saying he would appeal but would have to wait nine days. He would definitely get me released by then, he said.

He pulled out his cell phone and phoned my wife. While I wasn't allowed to speak to her, I heard her crying in the background. He told her to get confirmation of a place where I could stay and send the details to his office fax. He said that he would speak to her the next morning.

The time was around 8:00 p.m., I remember, and it was starting to get dark. For me, it probably seemed darker than it was. I succeeded in holding in my panic. I thought that if I let go then, I didn't know what would happen.

CHAPTER SIX

Maison d'arret, the First Twenty-four Hours

Without one word from the *gendarmes*, I was put into the vehicle and off they drove. I know now that it is only a five-minute walk and probably a two-minute car drive, but it felt like we spent an hour driving around the town. The arrogant *gendarme* said to me, "Do you like Limoges." I answered yes, but his sneering words that followed stayed with me for a long while. As we pulled up to the prison gates, he said, "Take a good look, this is the last you will see of it."

I had parked in the main town car park many times and had never really paid much attention to the wall of the prison across the road. But now, it looked so daunting bathed in the eerie, shadowy orange glow of the street lamps.

As we drove up to the orange-hued, grey steel doors, they automatically started to clang as they swung slowly open, flooding the area in an almost daylight white. We drove in through the large gates. There were two guards on each side of the vehicle with their hands poised on their holstered guns. It felt like I was watching an old 'B' movie

– gates clanging shut behind and in front as we advanced along the entrance corridor made for one vehicle.

We came to a halt alongside an old, thick oak door. With its black metal studs and hinges, it looked similar to the old Tudor entrances to Hampton Court Palace, it was obviously the original entrance into the prison itself. The guards waited for the large grey steel doors behind us to close automatically before I was hauled out of the car by my handcuffs. The two prison guards took charge of me, and the *gendarmes* followed behind.

I was hauled through the oak door and then, going up a step or two, through an inner, single steel door. I could see what looked like a ticket office with thick glass and a secondary office that was semi-open, like a shop counter. There on the countertop was already a "faxed" sheet with my details printed on it. With a handshake and a good deal of whispering, the *gendarmes* officially handed me over after the obligatory greetings. I was asked to hand over any personal possessions for storage and, although I didn't have to, I took off my watch and handed it to the translator. As it was a rare 1970 Omega Speedmaster that I didn't want to risk losing in prison, I felt that this was a good idea. I regretted the decision later, however, as I had no way of knowing the time.

The *gendarmes* just turned and left, beckoning to Frankie the translator. I was left with the guards to "process" me. A six-foot-tall man, smartly dressed in a suit but looking dishevelled, stepped forward.. "Who are you?" he asked in a deep voice worthy of his stature. I told them briefly who I was and why I was there. I also managed to get in that I was not guilty of the charges and that I thought I would be out of the prison upon appeal. They just shrugged, stating it wasn't their business.

The tall man surprised me by asking, "Is it your wife bringing charges?" He went on to mumble as he turned around to get paperwork, "It's usually an ex-wife wanting a divorce."

I had heard somewhere before that, in France, they were having problems with wives using the "my husband abused his children excuse" to get a quick divorce.

The man in charge spoke kindly, telling me that this would not be a nice place for me. On that charge, he was right. He put my charge sheet into a drawer and said that no one else other than those around now and the boss would see it.

He suggested that, should I be asked from this point why I was there, to lie and say "*escroquier informatique*" or, to you, "computer fraud."

This was probably the best advice I was to get generally. But one particular guard in this room was to take it upon himself to make my stay a little bit more interesting. I was then processed.

I am six feet tall but two guards, both taller than me, escorted me to a small room and told me to strip naked.

I was left for ten minutes to do so. On returning, I was subjected to a two-man body search. Leaning up against a wall while having my "orifices" checked invasively was humiliating enough in itself without having the two men involved, adding their own style of humor. Then, instead of handing my clothes back, the guards removed them, and I was left there standing naked for what must have been at least a half hour. But it felt like longer – a lot longer. Already exhausted, now cold and standing on a cold stone floor with nowhere to sit, I was fit to break.

Eventually, the guards returned. I was handed back

my clothes. Apparently, they had to be checked. I was also handed a bundle folded into a neat package that included a tray with cutlery, a piece of fruit, a piece of bread, and yogurt. I put down the bundle, ready to dress myself. "You can do that in the cell," I was told sharply.

This amounted to more humiliation control, I thought.

I was walked through the length of the prison. In my fear and anxiety, that picture has stayed with me until this day. When I close my eyes, I see it vividly. It's a culmination of all the prison films you have watched where a newcomer is walked through the center aisle to the sound of rowdy inmates banging cups on guard rails – the only difference being that all the cells were closed. By now, being about 10:00 p.m., it was fairly quiet, apart from the sound of rowdy inmates kicking doors or shouting.

The place looked like something out of an Edwardian period drama. The concrete floor was broken up, and I had to be careful where I trod. Above my head was a huge cargo net to stop things being thrown off the two floors above. The rows of doors were all solid and, due to the age of the prison, were only about one hundred sixty centimeters high with an eyehole to check on inmates.

I was walked through a second set of double gates to an area I was told was for "people like me." By that, I presumed that the area was sectioned off from the main inmates. I was told with a smile that I would only be safe until the next day, "when I would be put with the others."

I was almost pushed through the doorway, obviously having to duck quickly to get through. But, with the thickness of the walls being about one meter, I had to keep ducking until I reached the other end. The door quickly shut behind me with a clonk and a rattle of keys.

The cell looked tiny. I worked out later by counting floor tiles of twenty centimeters square that the cell was actually about four meters long by about three meters wide. It had a bunk bed, a toilet, a sink, and a polished-metal mirror. At the end of the bunk bed was a double-door (one on top of the other) wardrobe.

The shape of the cell was similar to that of a vaulted cellar. The ceiling was domed and covered in graffiti, boogers, and other unmentionables, and the floor was tiled. The only light was a tube above the metal mirror. Above that was an old clock that didn't work. There was a treble-barred window of about forty centimeters square. When I stood on a central heating pipe and look up at an angle, I could just see sky above, with a few stars in the light-polluted sky. There was a wall no more than about a meter away from the window. The window itself was about two and a half meters off the floor.

I familiarized myself with the cell. I had a look in the wardrobe, which was shelved out enough to put folded clothes on. I found an old battery and tried it in the clock. It worked, at least I could see the time. For some strange reason, seeing the clock work was like seeing a friend.

For the first night, at least, I was on my own. And, for the first time in three days, I had food, as little as it was. I sat myself down on the bottom bunk to put my clothes on and eat my food. I choked as I ate it slowly. It felt like a knot in my throat, and I gagged trying to swallow. Eventually, it went down. All of a sudden, the despair and loneliness came over me. It wasn't the situation that got to me, but the absolute loneliness. One can feel lonely and alienated on the first day on a new job or at a new school, but this was different. In a new job, within a few minutes you can make friends. I couldn't here. This was real isolation – physical and mental. Maybe I didn't even have a family anymore. I had to sort myself out. This was real, even though it felt like a dream.

The bed had a hard foam mattress, about fifty millimeters thick, and I had a blanket in my bundle, no pillows. I had to make up the bed.

I got on the top bunk and made it with the sheet I had, as I had no pillows. I stuck my shoes under the mattress to raise it slightly and lay down. I stared up at the dirty, domed ceiling until I dozed off. This was the first time in three days that I had slept, but it was short-lived. Every two hours, the guard would unlock the door and say my name. I was instructed to reply with "*oui servient*" to confirm that I was still alive. I was on suicide watch, probably a good thing at this point.

After the 5:00 a.m. check, I couldn't sleep anymore. I just lay there thinking, wondering how I ever ended up here. Never in a million years did I ever contemplate prison or these surroundings. A career criminal, I suppose, might contemplate such a thing and accept the risks. But having done nothing makes the scenario just surreal. On Monday morning, everything was fine. But, by 2:00 in the afternoon, it all fell apart. My mind was wandering again, trying to understand all the whys and the wherefores, until the sound of keys rattling in the door brought me to my senses.

It was 7:00 a.m., and the large, nasty guard was back on duty. He strolled into the cell, yelling as he went, "Get up! Get up, Greene. Your first day in pervert land."

"You will get up and dress ready for showers," he said authoritatively. He just stood there, waiting for me to follow his commands. I dressed in what clothes I had. I was escorted out the door and down about three doors on the left to what was a single shower cubicle. The guard stood outside. To shower, I had to push a button. The flow lasted about a minute before I had to push again. I showered, managing about four or five pushes of the button until the guard shouted, "*terminé*." I dried and dressed quickly before being escorted back to the cell, where I was locked in again. I could hear muffled voices and shouts of others being rousted for the same as everyone got up.

A minute or so passed, and I had just gotten up on to the bunk to relax when the servient returned. As he opened the door, he just shouted, "First day medical 10:00a.m."

I lay back on the bed with nothing to look at but the marked ceiling and, once again, nothing to think about but what I came to refer to as "the situation."

At ten minutes to 10:00 a.m., I heard the jangling of keys as the door was duly unlocked. With the words "Greene medical," I was beckoned out of the room and walked back down the center of the prison, the same route I had traveled to the cell the evening before.

This time, I was escorted up the center flight of stairs all the way to the second floor, passing other *servients* and the odd inmate on the way. I learned that all doors are locked at all times. There is no open time as you see on TV, where inmates can wander around. The doors are only opened for specific reasons. I will go into this later.

I was escorted to a *salle d'attente* (waiting room) and locked in to await the call of the nurse. It looked just like any other doctor's waiting room, with health-information posters on all the walls, mostly about drug use. It had a big window, barred on the outside, through which I could see a courtyard with a soccer pitch marked out on it. Over to the left side, I could see flats. I can remember thinking that these wouldn't serve as a very pleasant place to live, looking out of your bedroom window over a prison courtyard. My meanderings where interrupted by the guard unlocking the door. I was told to follow and was led into the "surgery" room.

The guard introduced me to a nurse and left the room, locking the door behind him. The nurse was dressed in white with a dark blue over apron. She was rather buxom and big-bottomed, but had quite a nice face. On her left cheek, she had a strawberry mark that she had tried unsuccessfully to hide with makeup.

She pointed to a dressing screen and, in a very high-pitched voice, told me to strip off and put a gown on, which I did. I was then subjected to a general medical examination, something like you would have received at school. She checked my hair, fingernails, tongue, mouth, teeth, blood pressure, heart, and lungs, then took an X-ray and asked loads of questions about what I do or don't do, such as smoke, drink, take drugs and needed medications, etc.

Eventually, all the paperwork was out and I was escorted back to the cell I had left. I was taken down two flights of stairs and handed back to Mr. Nasty to be escorted back to the cell.

As it was 12:30 p.m. and dejeuner is at 11:30 a.m., I had missed it.

"*Quel dommage,*" (what a shame) the servient said with a smirk on his face. This meant "tough luck," basically, so no food still.

As he left, he said, "*Rendezvous service socio 1400 heures*" (appointment with social services). My reply of, "*oui servient*" was a bit slow, so he banged the door with a fist and said in an indignant tone the words for me. He then locked up, leaving me to wonder what the bloody hell "*service socio*" was all about.

The time passed very slowly. It was only two and a half hours, but felt like four. Eventually, the keys rattled in the door, and it was time.

I was escorted again through the double gateway into the main area and was told just to wait at a door I had passed on the few times I had walked this path. Eventually, someone walked out of the room and a woman's voice said my surname.

I was met by a disheveled-looking black African woman sitting behind an office desk. She had a very pleasant, friendly smile. She told me to sit down in a very clear French-African lilted accent.

She asked me a few questions about how I was doing mentally and physically, if I needed anything, and whether I was being treated okay.

I explained why I was there, and also mentioned that I had been given hardly any food to speak of in four days. She was appalled. She immediately picked up the phone and called the chef. In a very stern tone, she told him that the situation was to be put right immediately.

I explained that I had only the clothes I stood up in, which didn't include socks, as I hadn't put any on the day I was "invited" to the gendarmerie.

She quickly scanned her paperwork to find that it said I was allowed no contact with Trudy or family until the judge gave permission. But she said she would contact Trudy immediately for me by telephone and tell her I needed clothes, etc. She also took the time to explain the "*bon command process*" (the opportunity to purchase items from a list) and that I would need money to buy provisions.

She explained that money sent in is held by the prison, and that we get slips of paper with provisions denoted on them to buy for ourselves – like soap, deodorant, razors, etc. Even things like cookies and chips were available.

On being processed, I was given a roll of toilet paper, a small bar of soap, and a shower gel sachet, but that was it until I purchased more supplies for myself.

I explained that I would only be here for nine days, as the avocat made an appeal to release me.

I asked her to tell Trudy that I loved her and that I was holding up. She said she would, and added that all I had to do was to ask the director (boss) for a service socio rendezvous if I needed to – and he couldn't refuse access.

I was then escorted back to the cell.

The *servient* walked me back to the cell. On arriving, he said with a sneer, "You have a friend," and laughed.

As the cell door opened, I was met by a retching smell. As I made my way into the cell, ducking, as one had to, to get under the low doorway, a guy of about sixty years of age jumped up and rushed at me with his head down. Shouting, he hit me square in the chest with his head and knocked me flying into the door the *servient* was just closing. The *servient* pulled his baton and took one big step over me, kicking me in the side as he went. He raised his baton and hit the smelly man twice across the side of the neck. He then dragged him out of the way and kicked me to get up enough so that he could get back out and lock the door, just leaving me to the mercy of this madman covered in shit and vomit.

I climbed onto the top bunk to get out of the way while the man recovered and got himself up off the floor. He looked up at me, shrugged, and said something that sounded

Russian in a very slurred way. He rummaged through his shitty trouser pockets and pulled out a piece of tinfoil. He obviously had not undergone the search I had due to his condition. He kept saying something to me that I didn't understand at first, but by his actions I gathered that he was asking for a lighter. He was obviously a crackhead just taken off the street, and I had the privilege of his company. It was going to be a long afternoon.

The keys rattled in the door, and a guard with baton ready appeared with the word "Greene." I jumped down and said "*oui servient*" keeping a eye on the unpredictable Russian crackhead.

He held out a small plastic tray with a sandwich on it. To the right of the tray was his baton, which I erroneously thought was at the ready in case the Russian should rush him again. But as I reached out to take the sandwich from him he used his baton and knocked it cleanly out of my hands. It landed on the ground and fell apart. As the guard stepped forward to demand the tray back, he squashed the sandwich into the ground with an "*ooplaa*" (French version of "whoops"). He was obviously offended by the demand made on him for some food, and made damned sure I wasn't going to eat it. He kicked the flattened mess of a sandwich back into the room.

The later part of the afternoon passed more slowly than the early part, as I was trying to keep out of the way of a very smelly crackhead who was slowly coming down off his high. The smell alone was enough to make me retch when I took a deep breath.

At 5:00 p.m., I heard the jangling sound of keys in the door, and the *servient* appeared in the doorway. He grabbed the Russian and led him away without a word. Five minutes later, the guard was back with a mop and bucket. He thrust these at me and said, "Clean your cell."

I had just finished cleaning when the keys rattled again and the door opened, with the *servient* declaring "*repas*" (dinner). I walked to the doorway without my tray and was told to go back for it. The tray I had been given on entry to this place had indentations for various foods. With a guard I hadn't seen before standing by, other inmates pushed the dinner trolley and dished the food. I queued up with four other inmates. It looked like my first meal would consist of two fish fingers, mashed potatoes, a Petits Filous yogurt, a chunk of bread, and a cube of Camembert cheese. I held out my tray, but the other three or four inmates were served first. As soon as they were served, they were hustled away. I was last, and for a minute I thought I wasn't going to get any. I held out the tray and, with a smile from the guard, I was dished up three fish fingers, two spoonfuls of mashed potatoes, and two chunks of French bread, as well as the other bits and pieces.

There was humanity in this place after all. The nasty guard had obviously been boasting about what he did to the "pervert," and this guard didn't agree with it.

I thanked him and turned to re-enter the cell. "Wait," someone said. I turned and was given a couple of sachets of coffee and four cubes of butter.

On re-entering the cell, the *servient* said "*bonne nuit*" (good night) and double-locked the door. This obviously meant that I was shut in for the evening and, once again, I was alone. Thank God – spending a night with the Russian was not my idea of fun. Not that there was any in this godforsaken place.

This marked the end of my first full day. Well, at least I

thought so – until at about 8:00 p.m. The keys rattled, and in walked the Russian, clean and tidy with a coverall on instead of his clothes. He was also a lot calmer and said to me in broken English, "I leave tomorrow."

Chapter SEVEN
Settling into a Routine

The cell security check continued every two hours throughout the night. I had no real time to sleep well, as with each check the keys would rattle in the door to double unlock and lock it, accompanied by the shout of "Greene" and the "*oui servient*" response expected of me. More of the same came at 6:00 a.m., but this time a rubbish bag, a coffee sachet, and slip of paper was added to the box on the door. As I was already up, I checked the slip of paper out. It was the Friday "*bon command*" order list, to be handed in by Sunday morning.

If I wanted any magazines delivered by the following Friday, I could have just ticked a box. But I didn't have any money, so that was no good.

Again, the keys rattled and the cell door opened, this time at 7:15 a.m., according to the old clock above the mirror. "Greene douche" (shower). Off I went to shower using the other shower gel sachet I received on entering. "Greene terminé" (finish) was called five minutes later.

On the way back to the cell, the nasty guard said simply, "*Rendezvous directeur 10:00 heures*" (appointment with the boss of the prison).

I got back to the cell to find that the mad Russian had gone. He wasn't too bad, after all. In our short time together, he told me his life story. I said early on that he looked to be about sixty years old, and I am usually good with ages. But I was shocked to find out that he was only forty-two, actually younger than me. The aged look had been brought on by vodka, prison, cocaine, and spending most of his free life travelling, looking for somewhere to settle. He made me sad. I pitied his life for that brief time.

He had spent most of his life in Pionerski in Kaliningrad, not far from Gdansk, Poland, as a fisherman. He came to Europe to make something of himself and so he could send money to his family, and ended up falling prey to the ugly side of France.

When there was no Russian to talk to, there wasn't much to do but lay on the bed and think. That's what I did until the keys rattled at 9:55 a.m. – on time for the director, I thought to myself.

I was surprised to find that the director who sat behind the desk was a woman. An attractive, slender, tall woman I guessed to be in her early fifties, she rose to shake my hand. She was wearing a power suit. "I don't blame her," I thought to myself. It must be hell in this 99.9 percent male environment. For a split second, I wondered whether the power-suit look would actually work in here. But, looking into her eyes, I would have said it wasn't just the clothing. Her eyes had a very cold, steely look to them. One look and one would wither in pain, I thought.

She introduced herself in a very formal manner, but I must say with quite a deep and husky voice. I looked down at her fingers to see that they were very nicotine stained. I thought, "That's where the husky voice comes from," as I sat there half-listening to what she was saying.

A man sat next to her who, after she had finished with the formalities, introduced himself as an educator. He had a very curly, wavy crop of hair that was as disheveled as you would imagine his type of hair would be. He even had leather patches on the elbows of his jacket, like a clichéd teacher. He spoke very slowly and precisely in English, and went on to tell me that he would translate for me if I needed something important or needed any assistance. I declined at this point, thanked him, and said, "I understand okay at the moment."

She pulled my file out from a few on her desk and glanced through it as though she hadn't looked at it before. People usually do this as a cover, so the person knows it isn't personal but "what the file says." Once again, I had to explain everything and made it clear that I was not guilty of the crimes. She explained some basic rules of the prison and asked if I took drugs or suchlike. She looked me in the eyes and said, "I don't think this place is for you. But while you are here, we will find you something to do." I said, "I would like that." She also told me I would be taken out of "isolation" after the weekend, which meant being put into main circulation and into another cell with an inmate.

I was once again told not to say anything about the offenses of which I had been accused, but to stick to the false story and make up enough to keep the inquisitive inmates informed.

She also signed me up for French lessons twice a week with the professor in the room with us. I would get a slip of paper under the door when there was a space in class for me. She asked if there was anything I wanted. I thought for a minute, and then asked for paper and a pencil if possible.

She looked at the educator, and he immediately rummaged through his case. He pulled out a folder, the type that has elastic on the corners to hold it closed. He checked its contents and handed it to me. It contained about four sheets of paper, a pencil, a pen, and an eraser.

She asked if the TV was working. I replied no, and she informed me that it is normally a paid-for service; but that she would have it switched on and would take the money later. It was fifteen euro per person, per month.

She bid me good day and rose to shake my hand. The educator rose from his chair at precisely the same moment, as he was leaving also. As I walked out the door, I said without thinking *"bonne journee,"* which means "have a good day," and then flashed her a look of apology. She replied with *"pareillement"* (equally), and a slight smile of acceptance.

The educator pulled the door closed behind me and put his hand out to shake mine. As he did so, he reiterated that, should I need help with the French, to just ask. I thanked him.

I was escorted back to the cell by the hovering guard. The clock above the mirror said it was an hour before *dejeuner* (breakfast). I can't remember what it was, but after having eaten only fish fingers and mashed potatoes in four days, it was great.

While I was eating, the TV came on!

The weekend passed very slowly, as I was on my own with only French TV for company. I put up with the endless game shows until *Prison Break Series 2* came on. How bizarre, I thought at the time – the whole prison had gone quiet, as they were all watching it, thinking the same as I was, no doubt.

It gave me plenty of time to think, not a good thing to do in prison. It made me angry and upset at the same time.

I tried not to think about home and what Trudy and the kids were doing. How were they handling Naomi? Did they believe her? Was I now alone – accused and condemned by my family and friends too? I always worry too much about how other people see me – a small insecurity in me, I suppose.

That weekend, I just lost myself in the room. I do not remember an awful lot, as I had to just shut down. Thoughts and questions with no answers were too difficult for me. Fear, anger, emotion, desperation, thoughts of the unknown, and, most of all, thoughts of the family I loved and cared about so much just felt like a handful of dust slipping through my fingers.

I have to say I contemplated the worst. I have always thought suicide was a selfish act, but at this moment in time, I had a right to be selfish and no reason to be unselfish, no reason to think of anyone else. The thoughts in my mind became real. With everyone against me and my whole life in turmoil, the misery set in and I couldn't snap out of it.

The servient visits numbered four hourly over the weekend and came only at night. During the day, they were pretty much nonexistent.

Could I do something and have enough time to die? The worst thing would be to get caught and survive. The way I would be treated would be worse, like a mental patient, like I was sick in the head, in a hospital ward chained to a bed.

I was good at problem-solving. This would be simple. It was almost "matter of fact" in my head. I wasn't sad about it at all, and it was all-consuming.

When I heard about the suicides of others, I would almost treat the acts with contempt, that the people somehow deserved to die. Never once did I contemplate the pain that led up to the acts.

Now I was that person, and I knew that all-consuming pain.

I remember wondering, like most people, I suppose, whether people changed their minds halfway through the act. But, judging by the way I felt at this moment, if they felt the same pain I was feeling, then they didn't. It just felt like it needed to be done. It would be a release from all this pressure, and whatever was waiting for me on the other side would be better than this, because they would know the truth. I have always believed in the afterlife and in my guides. They would be there to lead me away from this misery. They would put their arms around me and tell me all was well again.

In my processing pack, I was given a tray for food, a fork, and what looked like an open pen knife. The knife was not sharp, but the pack also contained two disposable razors. I could break them apart and use the little blade – that was possible. Sunday would be the best day, as everyone was lazy and there wouldn't be a full quota of staff, I thought.

It was also my last day on my own, as I would have a cellmate on Monday.

I was cold. It was mid-October and starting to get chilly. I had no socks on, as on the day of the arrest I hadn't put any on. That wouldn't help me if I cut my wrists. I needed to be warm. Maybe in bed it would be warm enough.

I got on with stripping one of the razors. The blade was very tiny, but I wrapped it in a piece of the Petits Filous yogurt package to make a handle.

I lay back on the bed, and the only thing I felt was heartbroken. Naomi had well and truly broken my heart, and all I could see was the anger on everyone's faces, looking at me as though I had committed this disgusting act.

Sunday came and, as predicted, was very quiet.

I was still resolute in my decision, and planned to act after lunch, when everything went quiet. The day was passing almost mechanically until the keys rattled in the door and the word "promenade" was bellowed at me. I didn't know whether this was a command or I could choose not to "walk," but I got up from the bed, put my shoes on, and followed the servient anyway. I was escorted almost to the entrance at the front of the prison, recognizable because I could see where I had been processed, and then we turned left. There was a line of inmates all being "frisked" and then let out of a door. I was about tenth in line. These were all inmates from the seclusion section, and the group looked to be a rough lot composed mostly of foreigners. I just kept my head down as I broke out into the sunshine, the first proper daylight I'd experienced in nearly a week. As I followed everyone else, I made for a back wall. The courtyard had a wall of about five meters high with barbed/ razor wire sloping inward. There didn't seem to be anything else beyond that I could see, apart from prison buildings and sky. I never thought the sky would be so welcoming. I had not really seen it properly since the arrest, apart from the bit when the gendarme van backed up to the door to escort me to the judge, and I can't remember even looking up at it then. I knew where I was in the middle of town, but there was nothing I could see to give me an exact position. I felt a bit like one does in the party game where one is blindfolded and spun around. I was so very disorientated.

One's mind always looks for something it recognizes, and if it doesn't find it, a mild form of panic sets in. I was having an inward panic attack. I wanted to run, but had nowhere to run to. I felt I would just run at a wall in the panic.

I needed to find a point of reference to slow down my brain panic and my heartbeat, otherwise it would turn into something physical. I looked up to see an airplane and a pigeon or two fly over. That was real. I concentrated on the plane and wondered where it was going, but I didn't even know where north, south, east, and west were, so I couldn't decide.

I looked back down to eye level to see people starting to walk toward me. In a split second, there was a flash of panic, but it quickly receded as they held their hands out to shake hands. No one said much apart from "*salut*" (hello, normally reserved for friends or equals), but everyone shook each other's hand. This was a rather bizarre but very French scene, actually, but was something I just didn't expect to see in a prison. A little bit of normality goes a long way, especially in this place.

As I didn't have a watch, I didn't know how long we were out in the compound, but it felt like hours. Realistically, it was probably an hour or so, and most of the time I stayed against the wall, not talking to anyone or making eye contact. There were a few activities going on, a couple of groups playing cards and another doing sit-ups and push-ups. A few inmates were just walking around the perimeter, but the major group was in the middle playing football, at least until one of them kicked the ball over the wall. That was the end of that. I half expected a row, but as the ball went over the wall, the inmates cheered. It was almost like they were happy for the ball to have escaped. Or was that me? Was that what I was thinking? The ball was anywhere but here in the compound with a load of criminals. What I would give to follow it.

I walked around the perimeter a few times to stretch my legs and decided it was about thirty meters by fifteen meters. I just kept my head down. Just then, a servient shouted something incoherent, but everyone filtered back to the door from which we had entered the courtyard. It was over – time to go back to the cell.

For my first contact with other inmates apart from those who delivered our sloppy dinner, it wasn't too bad.

Back at the cell, I put the TV on. I remember watching *Inspector Barnaby*. Now that was odd watching *Midsomer Murders* with French-dubbed voices that didn't sound anything like the original actors.

The "promenade" did me a world of good. For a start, I got some fresh air into my lungs, but it made me feel a whole lot different. I won't say I didn't think about suicide again, as that would be a lie, and I am sure my further feelings will come out as I progress with these writings. But suffice it to say that the promenade saved my life on that day.

Within an hour or so of getting back to the cell, the dinner turned up. It was the normal slop that, although not very appetizing, was better than nothing and necessary to curb the hunger pains.

I turned the TV off at about 10:00 p.m. I can't remember what I watched that last evening alone, as my head was not anywhere I would care to recall with glee. I remember crying again thinking about the family, thinking about a family I probably no longer had. I would like to say I slept, but over the time I had in the place, I could probably count on one hand the number of times I really had a full night's sleep.

CHAPTER EIGHT

Cell 16566

onday morning started routinely with rattling keys at 6:00 a.m. and doors along the line being unlocked. Then mine unlocked, opened, and a rubbish bag was added to the door pocket with my sachet of coffee and two butters. Of course, I had to say *"oui servient"* to confirm I was there and not missing or dead. After yesterday's escapades, I actually had a thought that the guard could have found me dead and I wouldn't be saying the words.

Shower day wasn't until Tuesday, so I got washed and shaved with my one good razor in cold water. I decided at this point to get rid of my beard, as I wouldn't be able to control it. This wasn't easy in cold water, but I managed it. Then I dressed and just stayed on the bunk and listened to the early-morning noises coming through the window.

At 10:00 a.m., the servient came to the door and said the words, "Greene, *directeur*" (Boss wanted a word), so I raised myself and followed obediently to the main office at the far end of the walkway.

Madam directeur, as we were instructed to call her, called me in and told me to sit. This time, no translator was present – just me and her. She was in a different power suit, but the same bored look was projected from those steely grey eyes.

She proceeded to tell me that at 1:00 p.m. I was going into main circulation, and again told me to get a story straight, as I would be asked many times why I was there.

She said, "I understand you are a psychologist?" I answered yes. She then went on to say that she was putting me in a cell with someone called "Bento Alexander," a very difficult inmate on morphine and other drugs due to being addicted to crack cocaine.

She apologized, but had nowhere else for me to go. She added flippantly that I may be able to help Bento, noting that he needed as much help as he could get.

With that, she rose and said, "You may go."

A sense of foreboding came across me as I was led back to my cell in solitary.

The dinner trolley turned up at 11:30 a.m. and delivered its normal slop, which I ate.

I made a cold-water coffee and, at that moment, it reminded me how much I missed a hot cup of tea.

I bundled up my belongings, sat on the bed, and waited. As 1:0 p.m. arrived, the key turned in my door. The guard said, "Greene, *demenagement*" (moving).

This was said really loudly, and it startled me at first. But, as I stepped out the door, I realized that the instruction wasn't just for me. As I ducked and left behind this shitty cell, I could see that all the gates in this area had been opened at once, and two *servients* stood at each gate. I gathered up my bundle wrapped in the bed linen and followed the main *servient*, who had his hand on his gun.

As each cell remains locked at all times, unless it's

dinner or a person is being let out for a rendezvous, I made the walk in almost quiet solitude. I passed only one other person as I was taken to the second level and what I knew to be the front of the prison.

I was stopped at cell number 16566 and told to wait. The guard walked over to a computer screen and tapped at it, then returned.

It was the same style door and made the same key noise as my previous cell. But on entering, I was met by the slight smell of paint. The cell had been cleaned and repainted. That was one good point. The cell was also slightly brighter, as I could see the sky at the top of the window – unlike the last cell, where all I could see was a wall. The toilet in this cell had sides and a door on the front. The door sat against the front of the toilet when no one was "on it," and it gave a modicum of privacy when one sat on the toilet, as it had to stay open and screened you from the rest of the cell.

I was handed a pack of disposable razors, a bar of soap, six sachets of shower gel, two rolls of toilet paper, and some toothpaste. I was told that was all I would get until I could buy my own. At this particular time, I thought I would only be here until the end of the week, as the nine days would be up and Maître M's appeal would release me. So these supplies would be more than enough!

I made myself comfortable, put my bedclothes on the top bunk, and there I sat. I realized that, if I perched up on my knees on the top bunk, I could see out the top of the window. For the first time, I also realized exactly where I was. I was at the front of the prison facing the car park. If you stood in the car park below, I was over on the right-hand side and in one of the top windows – in fact, the fourth one in. I could make out a road that I recognized over to my left, and I could see a BMW 3 Series waiting at the lights. I had to turn my head sideways and look through one eye to see, but at least I could see. The silence was interrupted by the clock tower chiming 2:00. I also heard a bus go past along the road that runs parallel to the prison. It was a veritable feast of urban information. I hadn't heard such noise for nearly a week, and it was good.

Within minutes, the keys rattled and in bundled Bento. He was tallish – not as tall as me, but skinny and gaunt-looking. His eyes were set close together with a monobrow above. He had a swarthy look to him, and I guessed him to be Portuguese or maybe Spanish.

He had the lolloping swagger of the gangbangers you see on TV. With red and blond streaks in his hair, he looked almost like a caricature. He already looked like a *Spitting Image* puppet from the TV series of the same name. I jumped off the top bunk to be polite and shake hands, but he just stared at me with a horrible look. His piercing gaze moved off to the top bunk behind me I had already made my own and, ignoring me completely, he reached behind me and pulled off all my bedclothes. I had made the bed quite well, so this pulled my mattress off, too. That got him mad, and, without saying a word to me, he fought and kicked the bed until it all came apart.

I guessed he just wanted the top bunk, so without a word I just picked up my stuff and put it on the bottom bunk. What more could I do?

Bento then spent the next hour huffing and puffing while making his own bed from the top bunk. When he eventually finished, he decided to pace backward and forward up the small gangway.

I just stayed on my bunk and kept my head down,

giving me time to figure him out a bit and decide how to deal with him. This was a good start, though!

He spent most of the day either pacing back and forth and/or talking to himself, using the word "*putain*" (bitch) an awful lot.

Dinner arrived at 5:50 p.m. Bento was on his bunk at the time, and he nearly landed on my head as he launched himself off onto the floor to race me to the door.

Rule one: Let him get to the door first at "*repas.*"

As usual, our trays had a dollop of whatever, and we were given our chunk of bread, coffee sachet, a Petits Filous yogurt or fruit compote.

A plastic garden table was in the corner in this cell, and by the time I got back in, he had already pulled it out and was sitting in the only chair. He was eating like a "Neanderthal" you see on a BBC documentary, just stuffing the food in his mouth by the handful. But, as there wasn't a lot of it, it was gone in about thirty seconds. He used his spoon to break the lid on his yogurt package like it was a boiled egg. That was gone in about ten seconds. Then he took mine! Before I had time to say anything, the lid was cracked and the package's contents were gone.

I said (in French, of course), "That was mine." He replied, "That's prison." I let it go this time.

Rule two: Don't leave food on the table.

He obviously felt like he needed to make an impression and play the hard cellmate. The trouble was, I had figured him out already.

He finished the first day as he had started it, taking charge of the TV by flicking channels and turning the sound up and down. When he wasn't doing that, he was striding back and forth shouting obscenities and kicking the door. This was just my luck, landing with a nut. I played my part, though, and just let him think he had made an impression.

He eventually went to bed at about 9:00 p.m., and I breathed a sigh of relief, at least until he started yelling from his bed at other noises in the prison. Then, every once in a while, he would jump down from the bunk and kick the door, with a "*putain* prison" shout, or suchlike.

So far, he had managed to spend all day in my company and had hardly even said a word. He went to sleep at about 11:00 p.m., and I thought that was it. But I had forgotten that people who snort cocaine do damage to their nostrils. I spent the rest of the night listening to him snoring. Not just typical snoring – this was the loudest snoring I had ever heard.

CHAPTER NINE
First Attack

I personally spent a very restless night. I was a bit wary of Bento, but was also kept up by lots of noises out front, including traffic into the small hours. Thankfully, the town clock bell stopped at midnight.

The usual routine of doors unlocking and things being put into the mailbox started at about 6:00 a.m. Then the "*douche*" call came at 6:45 a.m. I got my clothes on and followed the guard, one I hadn't seen before.

I walked in to find the shower area empty. The unit had three showers, each divided by a five-foot wall. I removed most of my clothes and reached over to push the button to start getting the shower up to temperature. The cubicle I chose was the first nearest the door, but before I had a chance to step into it, three other inmates walked in. I can remember thinking "one of them will have to wait" a split second before I realized what was going on. One guy stood at the door to keep an eye out while the other two pulled their towels from around their necks and, before I could say anything, one towel was around my face and upper body, held tight as my attacker twisted it. The second attacker got to the floor and wrapped his towel around my lower legs. It

69

all happened in a split second. I didn't have a chance. I was trying to shout out and kick loose, but they were holding me so tight I couldn't move.

Questions were thrown at me. Who are you? Why are you here? What cell? Why was I in the secluded section?

I have been in a few fights in my life, and I can honestly say that nothing up to this point had ever really scared me. But I had never been this scared. I just seemed to freeze. My bladder gave way, and I pissed myself. It just happened. The guy at my legs jumped back. I kicked out and caught him in the neck, and the guy with the towel around my face and shoulders fell away too. I called out to the guard, but no one came. I punched out at the guy falling away from my neck and caught him in the ear so hard he hit the shower divider. It took him a couple seconds to get himself together. The guy at the door had gone already, probably after I shouted for the guard. Then I noticed another guy coming into the shower. He dragged up the one on the floor who I had punched in the neck and kicked him out the door. The other one ran out after him.

My would-be savior reached out to me and put his hand on my shoulder. He just said, "*Ca va mieux*" (are you better now)?

As my eyes focused, I saw that he was light-skinned and looked Turkish or North African. He said he would hold the door while I got myself together. I stood in the shower for far too long and just kept pushing the button to restart the water. Eventually, the guard came around to the shower unit and shouted, "Greene *terminer*" (finish). I am sure he knew what had happened and just didn't want to get involved or, indeed, had something to do with it. I thought I had not seen him before, but I recalled that I recognized him from the first evening. He was one of the guards who had "processed" me. He smirked! The guy who had helped me had gone, too.

I went back to the cell, got on my bunk, and sobbed. Bento came in after his shower and didn't say a word.

I didn't report the incident to the *directeur*. I thought it best left unsaid and, apart from anything, I don't think I could even recall my attackers' faces.

Dinner came and went with the usual slobbering of Bento, and I just stayed on the bunk. At about 2:00 p.m., keys rattled in the door. Now I have mentioned keys rattling before, but if you want to understand more than the written words on the page, you have to hear them for yourselves. The sound produced a slight echo in the background. It started with a huge bundle rattling, then a key being inserted into the lock. This was not your neighbor's lock or one across the hall, but your lock. It was almost a pleasing sound. You knew in that instant that someone would appear at the door and say something. I dreamed the words " Greene *liberté*" (set free) many times, but soon came to realize it was usually something mundane, like "repas" or "promenade." Today at 2:00 p.m., it was something different – "Greene assistant social."

It was the black African lady again. I am sorry her name escapes me. "Sit down," she said. I obliged. She had a welcome and friendly face, and I burst into tears upon hearing the words, "How are you?" Again, the emotion of it all was getting to me. I couldn't even talk without crying. I explained what had happened in the morning. She said she would have to mention it to the *directeur*. But she basically indicated, "Don't hold your breath for a response."

I told her that I still had no money from home or change of clothes, and that I was cleaning my underwear every day and drying it on the pipe. At this point, she said she had contacted Trudy and told her that I was okay. She went on to say that Trudy was bringing in some clothes as soon as possible.

I felt good. My wife hadn't deserted me, .

The lady also handed me four stamped envelopes "for writing to *avocat* and other officials," she said.

I walked out of her office stunned, but with hope and a slight spring in my step. I could defeat this place – for the love of my wife back home, I could defeat this place.

I wasn't led back to the cell but was told that everyone had gone "promenade." So the guard took me to another set of doors, frisked me, and led me into a vestibule with another set of doors. The doors behind me were locked before the second set leading onto a courtyard with inmates milling around was unlocked.

I walked into the courtyard with my head down, trying to look inconspicuous. Men were pacing up and down the strip. I just went and stood in the corner, where I stood for what seemed like hours, but in reality was a half an hour. When the *servient* came back out and shouted, "Greene." God, he was calling me! I felt like the whole courtyard was watching me stride across to the door. I was frisked again and led to the *directeur's* office. I was questioned about what I had said to the assistant social. I told her what I remembered, leaving out the "pissing myself" bit, and she let me leave.

I was led back to the compound just as the servient decided it was time to come in. I was marched back to my cell, Alex Bento close behind. He followed with that surly look and slight left-sided grin, trying to walk with that same cocky stride but not quite getting it, and with that constant sniffing and hawking that gets to you in the emptiness of your cell.

Shortly after getting back in the cell, it was time for "*repas*." This breaks up the late afternoon/evening as, once you have eaten, you wash your cutlery and crockery and wait for the evening, when you can disrobe and get into bed. The act of doing that any day is quite welcome, as it ends another day. But after this morning's episode, it marked another day on which I was still alive, albeit laying in my bed thinking of my family. For the first time in nearly a week, I had heard that Trudy loved me and was waiting for me. I had two or three days to go and I could be out of this godforsaken, echoing shithole, I thought. In a place like this, even the echoes get to you. Shouts or muffled shouts your mind can deal with, but shouts and noises that reverberate and echo get drilled into in your subconsciousness.

CHAPTER TEN

Making Friends

Wednesday morning was uneventful. Bento, still his usual self, had pretty much ignored me and had certainly not introduced himself or even passed the time of day with me. He just sniffed and snorted during the day, with constant shouts, kicking of the door, and, when he felt the urge, adding the odd French expletive.

Dinner came and went and, at about 2:30 p.m., I heard keys in doors for promenade.

This time, I just filed in with everyone else. I was frisked at the entrance and filed straight through the two sets of double doors as they were guarded at both ends.

No guard stayed in the compound. But, as I looked up to the welcoming sunny sky above the five-meter (my estimate) wall, I noticed this time that there were two cubicles of glass with a guard sitting behind them, keeping watch over the compound and the grounds. I could just see CCTV monitors behind him.

Everyone filed around and did the "shake hands" thing that I found so bizarre the first time. I got to the promenade in a group. There must have been thirty or so men to shake hands with. I didn't really make too much eye contact, but just obliged with a "*salut*."

Bizarrely enough, Bento came and shook my hand with a "*salut voisin*" (neighbor). Close up, he matched the madman I had seen in him so far. He was monobrowed with very dark brown, looking almost black, eyes very close together. His nose was very long and looked very red compared to the rest of his swarthy look. He went off to shake hands with others. This was the first time he had actually spoken to me; I was polite and said, "Salut, Alex", using his first name.

The men seemed to be either walking around the perimeter or just back and forth over the length of the area, reminding me of caged lions pacing the wire. I started to do the same. I paced the outside perimeter with a natural stride, and found myself counting. This area, too, was about thirty meters long and fifteen meters wide, which amounted to about one hundred and ten footsteps, or a ninety-meter perimeter. There were quite a few other inmates doing the same, so I had to walk around those going slower or even those who sat on the floor with their backs against the wall. I noticed some playing cards and some doing other things, like swapping small items discreetly with a handshake. I pretended not to notice and just kept pacing.

I started to go back and forth instead of around and around, as it was easier to keep out of the way of anything I didn't want to see. I got into a routine of touching the walls at each end with my knuckles to mark the fact I got to the end. I don't know why, it just happened. I don't know how long I was doing this for, but I had fallen into a sort of routine trance, going back and forth so many times and knocking the wall that I had made my knuckles bleed. I resorted to a tap with my foot. I also worked out that if I counted how many round-trips I made, I would stay aware and could also create a future routine, knowing how much exercise I was getting. Walking the perimeter not too close to the edge gave me seventy steps, measuring about sixty meters, so it was better just to do the sixty meters going back and forth. Forty times would give me a kilometer walk, allowing for inaccuracy.

I walked to one end just as the *servient* opened the gate. I thought he was letting us out, but he was actually letting someone in. It was the guy who had helped me in the shower. He smiled at me and said "*salut, ça va maintenant*" (are you OK now)? I shook his hand firmly and thanked him. He introduced himself as Sheref. I smiled as I said his name sounded like "sheriff," as in "who shot the . . . "

"I know," he said. "I have English friends who say the same."

"Were you hurt?" he asked.

"Not really," I replied.

"It happens" he said. "Everyone wants to know your business to see if it benefits them or if it gives them power. It's the only power they have," he said.

We started talking for a while about what each of us was doing here, etc. He was a Turk, but had lived here for eighteen years. He went to Spain with a vehicle and got caught bringing a kilogram of cannabis back. He got two years, as it was a first offense. I felt sorry for him in a way. In the UK, he would have probably gotten a warning. Although he had been convicted, he was awaiting appeal and possible release with an ankle tag because his wife was about to have a baby. But so far, the appeal had been refused.

I told him I was in for computer fraud. It felt wrong lying to him, but I had no choice. I had already been attacked just to get information. God knows what would happen if it got out what I was really in here for.

Sheref had already been in here for eight months and knew a bit of who's who. He pointed out a few people to keep away from. One of them happened to be Bento. "No one likes him. He is a thief and will go through your possessions. He passes on information for a price, and he deals drugs in here," Sheref said. I was told how avocats are not searched and "can and do" pass drugs across. I had actually noticed that when the medic comes to the door with his concoction of pills, usually morphine, etc., and makes Bento take them in front of her/him, even though they check his mouth, he always comes back into the cell and spits something out. I have also seen him cut it up and sniff it up his nose or smoke it, although I have usually looked as though I haven't noticed anything. Sheref said that Bento also sells these for cigarettes, etc.

I asked if the three inmates who attacked me in the showers were present, and he pointed out the one who stood at the door. But Sheref said he was a gutless serpent who wouldn't do anything without his friends being there, and they were on a different wing so they wouldn't be on promenade at the same time as us. He did say that he didn't know why they were on the same shower run. I did –the *servient* had arranged it. I would bet on it.

Our conversation all ended too quickly. The *servient* opened the gate for us to file out and back to the cells.

I looked forward to seeing Sheref again. It was nice to talk freely after six days of not really talking to anyone.

Back at the cell, Bento went back to his normal self. He didn't like the sound of the keys locking him in. At the sound of them, he would get very frustrated and start talking to himself and smoking the cigarettes he had just bartered from someone. I much prefer for him to have a cigarette than not, as he is extremely agitated when he doesn't have any.

As he had made the effort to acknowledge me on promenade, at *repas* I tried to strike up conversation with him. But it wasn't very easy. I got out of him that he was in prison for drug offenses. This was his fifth time in a prison. He was Portuguese and had, this time, been given five years. But he was in this particular *putain* prison awaiting appeal.

He wished he was back in Toulouse prison or Clermont-Ferrand prison, as they were much better.

His conversation stopped abruptly as he barged past me to wash his food tray. That was all I got from him for the rest of the evening, apart from the normal farting, spitting, hawking, and shouting. Who said men can't multitask?

Thursday started quite uneventfully, until the servient came to the door at about 10:30 a.m. and said, "Greene professor." I followed him to a room at the far end of the prison to find a teacher and about three other inmates sitting around a table. It was time for my French lesson. This had been suggested earlier, but nothing had been mentioned since.

My lesson was quite enjoyable. An hour and a half away from Bento was good. Funnily enough, my French was ten times better than that of the other three. One of these men was Russian and looked as battered by drugs as anyone could be. The other two were Portuguese and not very bright. The lesson ended all to soon, but the upshot was that the professor gave me another folder containing half a dozen sheets of plain paper, an exercise book, a pack of pens and pencils, and an eraser .

I arrived back at the cell in time for lunch. Bento was more interested in what I had brought back from my lesson, and picked the folder up off the table. I had been warned that he noses through things. I slapped my hand on the folder so he couldn't pick it up and sharply said "*laissez*" (leave it). He just stared at me for a few seconds, then just snickered.

I sat on the bunk in the afternoon and wrote to Maitre M to ask how things were progressing, especially as today he would be able to lodge the appeal. At this point, I was still hoping and believing that I may be out by the next day. I hadn't heard anything from Maitre M, which annoyed me a little.

Mentally, I was handling the situation, albeit with waves of emotion and dread at times. After the incident in the shower, I knew the guards would not protect me. I think they would be party to anything that went on, and suspected that the danger would be coming back. If I knew one thing, I knew that. I don't know why, but I just felt it was a matter of time. Maybe tomorrow would be the end of it, and I would be out of this place.

Whatever happened, I felt a little stronger. I had been attacked, and I had survived it pretty much unscathed – with thanks to Sheref, too, of course. But I actually felt stronger inside. The unknown was now no longer unknown. Do you understand that feeling?

Ironically enough, on Thursday evening a double episode of *Prison Break* was to air, so both Bento and I went to our bunks to watch it. The show was not without its interruptions, of course. Bento thought he would exercise his imaginary authority and kept turning the TV to another channel during the advertisements, not turning it back for five minutes. He would either do that or turn the TV to mute so he could yell at someone outside or in another cell. I let him do it without a word. This was not out of cowardice, you understand – it just wasn't worth causing trouble over. I was locked in a cell with a crackhead without crack, and the guards would not help very quickly if "he went off on one." Bento fell asleep during the second episode, so all was quiet.

On Friday, I got up with a positive feeling, thinking that I might hear something today. I remember thinking that the previous night could have been my last in that bunk.

Shower was called at 7:00 a.m. as usual, and that passed without a hitch. It's amazing how good it makes you feel to be under the water to wash the grime of prison away. The only thing that breaks the feeling is that the button has to be pushed every thirty seconds to keep the water running.

Promenade was called at 9:00 a.m., and I can remember even now that it was getting colder outside. This was even more noticeable since I didn't have anything but a shirt to wear.

Sheref was there, and I walked around with him for a while, getting to know a bit about his private life. His wife was pregnant and due in a week or so. She had been taken into the hospital, so he was hoping to get out to see her.

I didn't crowd him, as he had friends in the yard. He had introduced me to a few of them. One particular guy called Yannick spoke a little bit of English, the basics. But he said the words he knew with a smile. It was nice to hear. Actually, it was nice to see someone smile. He was a very amiable chap. He was also very short, probably no more that five feet tall, and was very French with a good suntan. I couldn't tell whether it was natural or not. He always wore a baseball cap as well as that smile. Apparently, he stole cars for others to make money.

We shared stories about how we got here. This was a common question every day. There was no backslapping over what you had done. The subject was just an icebreaker. No one was really interested past the first few sentences of your explanation, unless it interested them for another reason. I learned to "see that" and to know when to stop. It was easy for me, as I could just say I didn't understand the question.

I expanded on my story just enough to "get me by." I said that I was in there for computer fraud, taking money from big companies. At first, I was questioned as to why I was in this place for something like this. It wasn't normal to be imprisoned for such a thing, but I had the fact that I was English on my side. I was a "flight risk." That seemed to soothe their curiosity, thankfully. Even with the language barrier, they could tell I wasn't the normal sort of prisoner. They always asked about family, too, and that hurt. I would say happily, "Oh yes, I have a wife and three children." I would then have to describe in detail who they were. In the back of my mind, that always felt worse than the computer fraud lie. It always dragged up hurt and loss.

We read, see films, and hear news stories about prisoners all the time, and we only ever look at them as "prisoners." Yes, there are some hard criminals who have no difficulty in hurting others. But some are just people who have gotten themselves into trouble. Some are just like me, innocent in a place of captivity and having no way to prove it.

One thing unites us all, and that is that we are still all human beings. The French "maison d'arret" is a halfway house, a remand prison. It has never been and probably will never be funded properly, so it will continue to be no more than a cattle shed in disrepair.

The shout to go back to the cell always caught me unaware. I was usually in my own little world somewhere, enjoying the air.

We got back to the cell at about 10:30 a.m. Bento hadn't

gone on promenade and was up at the window responding to someone whistling. I remembered at the time that it sounded like my wife's whistle.

I had only been in for five minutes when the keys rattled and a guard called "Greene" and threw a black sack at me. I opened it to find clothes. At long last, my wife had sent me clothes so I could change. I was rummaging through the bag, and I found two A4 (similar to letter size) sheets of paper. On each one was a black-and-white photo, one of my wife, the other of my wife and me. Written around the outside was, "I will always love you, and I am waiting for you." This was the first word I had heard from anyone, let alone my wife. I was totally overwhelmed. This was the first indication of support I had received. There WAS hope. She STILL cared about me. She STILL loved me. She WAS waiting for me to come home. There WAS hope. I cried clutching the photos. Bento didn't even pay attention. He was looking out the window. I just cried. In an instant, everything had changed. I was still in here, but I wasn't alone. There it was, written in black and white.

I lay on the bunk and stuck the pictures on the spring section of the upper bunk so I could look up at them. She was waiting for me. I knew I could be stronger now. I had reason to go home.

That whistle, it was Trudy. But she had gone by the time I realized it could have been.

I also got a message from the *directeur* saying that money had been placed into my account, so I could pay for the TV and buy something with those "*bon command*" slips that get left in the post box.

I had a look at the current day's slip, which had to be placed in the box for Saturday morning for goods to be delivered by Tuesday. I thought I might not be here by then, but took the chance anyway.

I ordered a packet of cookies and, although I didn't have a kettle, a small packet of tea, two packets of tobacco (as advised by Sheref) as a bargaining tool, and lastly a proper notepad so I could at least write something. I love to write, and it calms my spirit when I'm emotional or distressed.

I stayed on the bunk most of the day and thought of home, wondering what was going on there and, if my wife was on my side, what was happening to Naomi. I imagined it to be hell. They must all be distraught, except Naomi, of course. But, then again, not if Trudy had her claws in.

For some reason, I thought of my dogs, as I did miss them. I thought of Ariel, the little cocker spaniel. She loves me dearly, I thought, and she must be missing me too.

In a millisecond, my outlook had changed. I had something to go home to. The song "Home" by Westlife came to mind. But then I cried again.

I pulled myself out of the memory trip and changed into the new clothes my wife had brought in for me. Memories hurt too much. The day finished without hearing about the appeal from Maitre M. The weekend was upon me.

Saturday was quite quiet, as most of the staff had gone home and only necessary staff stayed. I had to put up with Bento grunting most of the day. He had managed to save some of his medication. He broke one of his razors into pieces and started chopping at the pill until it was a fine powder. He was quite adept at this. He then snorted the fine powder up his nose and also made up a cigarette with it and smoked it.

It kept him quiet for the rest of the day, and he slept a lot. Saturday French TV is full of game shows, but in the evening a couple of films came on. I remember seeing the *Miami Vice* film. I wonder whose job it was to match French voices to American faces. He needs the sack, whoever it is!

I think Thomas Edison said that, "Necessity is the mother of invention." In my boredom, I was thinking about the tea I ordered, and I had an idea.

Every day, we got a foil cup of mashed fruit compote. I had saved a few because Bento would occasionally, when he could be bothered, use them as ashtrays. I had also saved about a half dozen little packs of butter. After a week and a half in this shithole, I wanted a cup of *hot* tea or coffee.

I put a pack of butter on the radiator pipe and, although it was only lukewarm, softened the butter in about an hour. I soaked a tissue from a packet of tissues in the butter. It took another hour to soak up. It was a slow process, but if it worked, it would be worth it.

I got one of the foil fruit cups and cut a hole in the bottom, put holes in the side with a pencil, then turned it up the other way and sort of crimped it together with another by cutting slots in it.

What could I use as a kettle?

I remembered that in the cupboard was a little round can that originally had cashew nuts in it. This would be ideal, *but* Bento had staked a claim on it and used it for his tobacco and other smoking implements. He had seen me busying myself with the compote cups but didn't say anything. I thought about just taking it and tipping his stuff out, but thought better of it. I asked him if I could borrow it to make hot water, and he grunted in agreement, as long as he could have a cup if it worked.

I rinsed it out first. I lit the butter-soaked tissue with Bento's lighter and stood it on the window ledge. I then stood the can on the top. It smoked a bit, but opening the vent on the window helped it a little.

I checked it every five minutes. It took about twenty minutes to get hot, but get hot it did! I made my first hot coffee in nearly two weeks. God was it was good!

Bento, in his stupor, looked impressed and pointed at his chest as a, "Me too?" He was never one for many words. I made one for him. This was something so simple, but a revelation to us both – a hot cup of coffee. Now all we had to do was save foils and butter. What I would give for a couple of tea light candles!

Chapter ELEVEN
The Second Attack

Sunday started early with the door keys rattling for "shower." On this floor, normally about three cells are called. That's six men, as there are two shower units on this section with three showers each. But I only remembered our door being unlocked! Not really thinking about it, I half-dressed and went off to the shower. Bento didn't follow, as he was talking to the guard. I got into the empty shower room and started undressing. I looked up as I saw two men walk in and, in a split second, my heart sank as I realized it was the same two inmates who had attacked me before. I had seen one of them in the yard on promenade and, apart from eye contact, nothing had been said. I thought maybe they had just come for a shower, but they edged toward me with a look of no good in their eyes. I backed up but stumbled, as my trousers were around my ankles. I shouted for the *servient*, but heard nothing. There was no one else around – this was a second setup. I tried to get to my feet, as at least I could do something to protect myself if I could get up. But one of them stood on my trousers so I couldn't right myself. It's only now that I think about the voices that I recognize the questions, but at the time they sounded muffled. My fear had scrambled the shouts and demands as I was listening to my mind telling me to get up, protect myself, and call for help.

The questions sounded like: "Who are you? What are you doing in here? Answer me or I will kill you. Do you want to die?"

The big one, who I now know was a Russian, said, "There is no one here to help you, you are mine" I tried to call out and, as if he knew I was about to yell, he punched me in the throat to keep me from yelling for the guard. It worked, but adrenaline took over, and I was fighting the Russian away. Then another two men came in. One carried what looked like a large towel, but I think it was a white bed sheet. Within seconds, it was around my neck and face. I writhed and kicked out but seemed to be kicking at air as I could no longer see them but only hear them. One of the men punched me hard in the kidney and then in the stomach. I couldn't resist any longer as I was choking already. I couldn't breathe in or out and just slumped. I felt like I was passing out. The sounds around me were muffled as if I had my head in a bucket, but I just heard one say, "I don't care about what I don't know." At first I thought I was being hauled to my feet. However, the sheet was being twisted and all I could do to stop my neck from being twisted too far was to follow it and turn myself over, it was then that I realized what was happening, my trousers were being pulled off from around my feet and my underwear ripped off.

I tried to struggle but felt heaviness around my arms and my legs. My head felt like it would explode. I was so weak I could no longer struggle; a black ring surrounded my outer vision looking through the white light of the sheet as my face was being pushed onto the cold tiled shower room floor. I could just hear the sounds of my attackers talking, interspersed with what sounded like laughter.

I knew what was happening, but I tried to block it out. I could feel the man's penis on my buttocks and braced myself in my head for what was to come next. I tried to clench my buttocks together but it was not working as the man just pulled my legs apart, I felt his weight then I felt the pain as he inserted and thrust at me from behind. I do not know whether I blacked out or my mind deleted the pain from here on but the next thing I remember was being hauled to my feet. I am quite big, so it must have been like lifting a deadweight.

With the centre of the sheet wrapped around my neck and the lower part of my face like a scarf, now covering my mouth, the men looped each of the ends of the sheet around a window bar higher up, enabling them to almost winch me up using the bars. My feet left the ground as I struggled as best I could. I felt my neck stretching with my body weight pulling down. They just tied the sheet and, as quickly as they could, they disappeared out the door.

I wasn't physically panicking, but was panicking in my head. I felt my eyes bulging, and my vision started to go black around the edges again. I was only a couple of centimetres off the ground, but it may as well have been a meter. In my head, I thought I was just going to die hanging here. But I had to fight on. As quickly as I thought I might die there, I thought *no*! I have still got good, strong shoulders, and when I was training, I used to lift weights hanging down my back. I would try and get my hands up to the bar. I could hold my own weight and stop my neck from stretching any more. I managed to get one hand up, which allowed me to turn slightly. As I did this, I kicked something. I had forgotten about the rubbish bin in the corner. Using this momentum again, I managed to bring the bin closer to my feet while holding the bars behind my head with both hands. It would have been better to turn it over, but this was all in a few seconds. With a burst of panic strength, I managed to pull both feet up, letting them rest on the sides of the metal bin's edge. I couldn't lift myself out of the sheet, but it took some of the strain off my neck. Unfortunately, I only got relief for a split second as the bin flattened with my weight on it. Even in its flat state, it was enough to elevate me a couple of centimetres. It gave me breathing space for what seemed like a few seconds. My vision was going black, and the exhaustion was winning over the effort to hold myself up. I felt myself slipping and my neck stretching again. Then, all of a sudden, I could hear a commotion. But I couldn't see. A guard had come in and punched an alarm on the wall outside the cell at the sight of me hanging there naked, and within seconds there were three or four guards lifting me out of the sheet.

They sat me on the floor, speaking words I couldn't understand. I remember being wrapped in what looked like a silver blanket, but I wouldn't trust my muzzy head. The guards around me seemed to be moving in slow motion and talking in what sounded like an alien language. I wasn't with it, and I couldn't move for a very long time.

I remember eventually being taken to the infirmary, where I was cleaned down with a gentle touch, I stayed for the rest of the day feeling pain in every part of my body.

I cried, I stared into space and I cried some more, all I could feel and hear all day was that man.

The *directeur* came in to "have a chat." I mentioned that

the guard had left me in there and that I thought he had done so on purpose. She said she would look into it. I saw a flash of emotion in her normally cold grey eyes as she got up and put her hand on my arm

I never heard anything more on the subject the entire time I was there. "That's prison," I was told more than once by more than one person.

I was asked if I wanted my wife contacted about the matter but declined. She was already under stress, and my contacting her would have made matters worse for the both of us.

I was returned to the cell at about 5:00 p.m. Bento, as usual, said nothing, and I wouldn't be surprised if he had been a part of the attack.

I was still a bit sore around the neck and back, and the backs of my arms were bruised and sore. I looked at myself in the steel mirror and, although it doesn't give a good reflection, I could see there were very few marks, mainly just what the sheet had left. I felt emotion again and just sucked it back. I was angrier. I just paced the room a bit finding things to do. I checked through my "stuff." There was not much, but it was there and it was mine. I suspected it wasn't where I had left it. Bento had been through my stuff, but I didn't fancy a confrontation. I might have lost it and done something I would have regretted. It could wait – he would do it again for sure. I would just make sure it was a bit more secure, if that was at all possible.

I eventually got into bed at about 8:00 p.m. and lay on my good side, trying to blot out the day's events, which wasn't very easy. Every time I closed my eyes, in my mind I was either hanging from a towel or on my front on a cold floor. The bruises heal, the physical pain goes but still to this day, that nightmare comes back on a regular basis. It is only recently that I have managed to tell anyone, including my wife what really happened on this day.

Monday morning came early, even though I didn't really sleep much, just a few minutes here and there. The church bell started ringing at 5:00 a.m., and all I could do was to lie there and listen. I didn't sleep well at all, as every time I closed my eyes, I was hanging by my neck from a sheet. The pain while trying to lie in a good position probably prompted the memory. This particular Monday morning was just the beginning of a bad day. The guard rattled keys as always, but this time there was mail for me. It was from Maitre M. I opened it with haste, thinking it might be news of the appeal, and indeed it was. I had to read it a couple of times, but the gist of it was that the appeal had been refused. I was stunned into silence – devastated is not a word I could use, as every part of my body froze. Maitre M had assured me everything would be well, and it wasn't. I was stuck in this place now without any hope of release. I can't describe in any words how it made me feel. Even writing about it gives me a shiver just remembering the words. Half of me was trying to pull myself out of the numbness, telling myself I have to survive. The other half of me was immersed in the terrifying thought of staying in this place for twenty years. The words of that damned woman judge rung through my ears – "I am going to put you away for twenty years." She would succeed if this farce continued to the end, with the authorities listening to Naomi's accusations and believing what she was saying and not me. I would not see the outside again.

I cannot write what I felt this day. The emotions, fears, and feelings were too deep to put into words. I am quite an emotional person and can cry quite easily, but I couldn't even do that. Thoughts of suicide flashed in and out of my mind. Even the attack made me angry again. If they had succeeded, I wouldn't be in this pain now.

I had to take control. I felt like I was rolling down a hill, just getting faster and faster out of control. I jolted myself out by shaking my head. I thought for a second. I told my mind to shut up, shut up, shut up, shut up! Eventually, I managed the presence of mind to put myself into one of my controlled semi-meditations to control my anguish. I had to, as I felt weak and vulnerable at the same time. Then, out of the blue, I heard the keys rattling along the corridor and in our door. The guard appeared and shouted, "promenade." It was past 10:00 a.m., and I had been "out of it" for upwards of an hour. I shook my head again, logic took over, and I decided to go out, especially as Bento had decided to stay in. I wanted an hour away from him, and a walk would do me some good, clear my head.

Those who meditate in any way for balancing, energy control, or just relaxation will know that it tends to heighten senses, especially when you come out of it quickly like I just had to the "promenade" command. I got outside into the open, and I can remember it being crisply cool, but with the sun out. I had previously noted that, at this time in the compound, the sun creeps down the right-hand wall. But it wasn't quite low enough to enjoy, as it was probably three meters up. So I walked. I walked around and around the perimeter. I think I continued the meditation, because I don't remember much after five or six laps, but I continued to walk. I didn't see Sheref, but Yannick came over to me and broke my trance. He said to me, "It's not good to be on your own in here, English. Come and walk with me."

I did so for a few laps and had a bit of a chat. But I was so focused out in the open that I didn't speak a lot, and he gradually wandered off. I noticed the sun had crept to about a meter off the floor, so I went and stood against the right wall. Putting my head against the wall, I looked up and drew a few rays of sun.

So far, I haven't mentioned the prison pigeons. But I think I should, as they have made a very definite impression on my thoughts. Every time I see them, even now, in close proximity, I get a "prison flashback." I wouldn't say I hate them, for it it's more of a "love- hate" thing. Let me explain.

Within the prison walls, you can hear them and see them whether you are in the cell or in the compound. In the cell, they sit on the edges of the windows and make that damned cooing noise all the time. But it is in the compound that I remember them most.

The right-hand wall I mentioned, the one that gets the sun gradually moving down it, is the main cell wall. It is full of cell windows, and the inmates tend to throw their waste food, mostly bread, out into the compound. This brings in the pigeons.

If, like me, you walk the perimeter, or even walk backward and forward, they are always on the ground eating, and are always in the way. They fly up as you reach them and fly back down as you pass – either that or they just run around your feet. I didn't kick any, but the urge is there. I have seen one or two pigeons kicked out of the way by an inmate, occasionally killing them in the process. There is a contrast to this – at least for me there was. They fly freely around the compound cooing at each other from up on the wall, and I found myself slightly jealous. Yes, I did say it. I was jealous of a pigeon. When you are confined like I was, sometimes the only relief from the solitude of the hard, stone walls is to look up. The pigeons represent a freedom of sorts, just freely flying up over the top of the wall. This is just what I wanted to do this very day and every other day while walking this compound – start running and just fly as far away from here as possible.

Airliners flew over too, and the thought that they were full of free passengers, again going on or coming back from vacation, made it worse.

Once again, I was abruptly shaken out of these thoughts by the guard calling us back in. Back to reality, and back to the cell for the rest of the day.

Bento was on his bed facing the wall. I got in and went to the wardrobe, where I had put the letter from Maitre M. I wanted to read it again. I don't know why, I just had to read it again. I noticed it had moved. Bento had been going through my things again. This time, I was not in the mood for reason. I grabbed him by the back of his shirt, and he rolled toward me. I think he must have been sleeping, because he jumped up with a start. I dragged him off the bed and onto the floor. He landed on his feet, and I waved the letter in front of him and shouted at him to leave my stuff alone. I shouted in English though, as I was angry, but he got the drift. He looked at me with an odd look. For the first time, I saw vulnerability in his face. For all his times in prison, he had fear in his eyes. I pushed him away. From now on, I needed to be more careful. As far as I knew, no one knew why I was really here, and some of my paperwork contained codes that people might recognize. He got back up on his bunk, and I got on mine. Nothing more was said.

I wanted this day to end and bring Tuesday, to start

another day with a fresh mind.

In my own words, I had to "get a grip," put the attacks behind me, and deal with the fact that I could be in here for years. It was only midday, though, and still at least eight hours before I could go to bed.

Keys rattling brought *dejeuner.* I hoped today I could manage to swallow some food without too much pain. When dinner or lunch was served and when it was shower time, the guards always unlocked our door and the next-door neighbor's. They were a funny pair. They always seemed the best of friends, and always came out of their cell laughing and chatting. Often, you could hear them through the walls mumbling and laughing. I know they used to get cannabis resin in, as they offered it to me once. And we always managed to have a quick chat.

They were complete opposites to look at. Philip was very French with a very Napoleonic nose. He was also deformed in the back with a twisted spine. It must have affected his voice box, too, as he had a very deep, gravelly voice for his small stature. But he was always smiling. Lucas, however, was a Tom Cruise look-alike. He just seemed as though he would glide around on wheels and was always smartly dressed, albeit in tracksuits and sweatshirts.

As they came out today, they gave me a look of concern and asked if I was okay. They asked with a few expletives about how the attack could have happened. I assured them I was fine, physically at least.

I took the opportunity today to ask Philip if he had something like a small tin and explained why. Luckily, he did. It was a drinking chocolate mix tin – just the thing to boil water in, as long as it was water tight, of course.

He said he had a kettle that he had bought on his

"*bon command*," but the list for things like this only come every three months. He went on to say he would have a boiled kettle ready during shower mornings, so when the guards left the door open while we showered, I could swap a cigarette for a cup of hot water. This was a great idea, I thought. I shook his hand on it, but it also depended on whether the guard on duty at the time would allow this, so I wouldn't hold my breath. The guard on this day was fine and let us chat a little. The food servers did their job more slowly, too, rummaging for bread in the bottom of a bag to give us more time.

The afternoon went very slowly, interrupted only by a couple of cups of coffee with my new tin. It was good and didn't leak. I didn't offer one to Bento this time.

One of the good things about being on the bottom bunk was that I could use the frame of the top bunk as an exercise board. Holding onto the sides, I managed about twenty pull-ups per rep using my arms and keeping my body stiff. In between, I got up and paced the floor, about five steps each way.

Today, I felt like screaming out. The roof felt like it was a heavy weight on my head. I know what it must feel like to drown, I think. I felt like I couldn't breathe, like I was suffocating. I opened my mouth and let out a silent scream. That's all I could do after the events of the last two days, scream silently.

I put the TV on at about 4:40 p.m. and watched Rex, a program about a clever police dog. It took my mind off the cell room, but it made me think about my dogs and how much I missed them. I might never see them again, as they would all have died before I left prison.

Evening *repas* came and went in the usual way and,

thankfully, eventually it was time to retire to the bunk.

Today I had no more fight in me. I was slipping into a "protect myself by being negative" mode. If anything good happened, it was a bonus. My wife is like that normally, always thinking the worst of a situation, any situation. She did this so that if anything bad happened, it was half expected, and if anything good happened, it was even more exciting. I now know how she felt and why she did that. I have come to terms with a lot of stuff in here. It's amazing how sharp things can feel when you have your liberty taken away.

I had a treat today, too. I boiled up some water and poured it into the washbowl. For the first time in nearly two weeks, I washed in slightly warm water. I washed and shaved almost ceremoniously to end the day. Bed became a release for me, as it ended one day and started another with, hopefully, a few hours of oblivion in between, if I could actually manage to get to sleep long enough.

Tuesday morning came early with a rattle of keys and "douche" shouted at me. At the thought of it I went cold. But I had to get on and do it. This time, I chose to hang back until there were others showering or preparing to do so. I also chose the shower on the other side of the walkways and found two of them occupied. Not that it would help much if something did happen, but I would have company – safety in numbers and all that. It was, however, uneventful, and I was washed and out in five minutes. I went back to the cell and shaved in cold water, but at least my face was softer from the hot shower, so it didn't rasp so much. I had just finished and dressed properly when the guard called "promenade." The usual checks and frisk-down felt a little lighter than normal. I think they knew I had bruised and sore parts. Oddly enough, these didn't visually show too much, although they were still giving me pain. But I found out that that's why towels and sheets are used, so as to mask the blows enough to not leave marks.

I was met by Sheref and Yannick, who came straight over to me to see how I was. It was nice to know someone cared in a place like this – not just about me, but was just human enough to care about anything. To most in here, caring was a sign of weakness. Most were just like caged animals with nothing to do.

Yannick complained that I hadn't told him what had happened when I met him yesterday on promenade. Then I had to explain what had happened. It clearly made Sheref especially angry. He was hurting also, as he had news that he was not allowed out to see his wife give birth. "Prison has no heart," he said with a tear in his eye.

Later on in the conversation, Sheref asked how I was getting along with the "*dementi*" (slang for mad person). I gathered that this meant Bento, but frowned at the word. He then said "lunatic Alex." I proceeded to tell him that he had been through my private papers. Sheref called over someone I didn't know to speak to and explained what I had said. It was Bento's old cellmate who had asked for him to be removed. I thanked him for that, rather sarcastically, and he said that if Bento hadn't been moved he would be dead, because the cellmate had endured enough of the same treatment I was getting. Private possessions are everything in here.

I even mentioned that Bento had taken my coffee, butter, and bread. The chap whom I came to know as "Elvis" said he had experienced the same. He said that I needed to stop him, otherwise he would just get worse. I asked what I could do to stop him, and the answer was not what I wanted to hear.

In basic terms, I had to be violent with him. I said I can't get violent over a few sachets of coffee, and Elvis just shrugged and said, "*Comme vous voulez*" (As you wish.). Trouble is, I knew it would be. I knew it would come to that.

Before I had a half hour of promenade, the keys rattled at the gate, and I heard the call "Greene." It always sent a chill down my back, wondering what it was I was in for now. Always single words, this time it was "*directeur*." I was frisked as normal and then escorted to the director's office.

This time it was the male director. I think there must be two or three, but I smiled to myself thinking it was like a pub restaurant in the UK run by a husband and wife team!

Before I even had time to sit, he asked me how I was and if I needed to speak to anyone. He then added, slightly quieter, that it would be better if I didn't, "Yes, I bet it would," I said. It's at times like this that I wished I could rant in French in the way I could in English. As I got up to go in disgust, I turned back and spat the words at him. "It wasn't you who was raped and that nearly died being strung up to a window bar, was it?" He surprised me as he said in English, "Sit down, Monsieur Greene."

I mumbled under my breath, "Now you speak English."

"Yes I do, Monsieur Greene," he said indignantly.

I said straight to him in English, "If you just want to keep this quiet, why am I here?" I couldn't believe my own words, really speaking like that to the director to whom everyone kowtows, but I was angry and upset. I didn't sit, but just stood with my hands on the back of the chair.

Ignoring my "outbreak," he proceeded to tell me that the man concerned was Russian. He was already in here for murder, so punishing him would not help matters. But he had been transferred now to full prison, and the other two who helped him were in another area where I would not bump into them.

"What about the guard that set me up?" I asked. He totally ignored the question and changed the subject in an instant.

"Would you like to work, Monsieur Greene?"

I agreed that this would be a good idea. He would suggest it to the "*chef de cuisine*" that I would like to work in the kitchen. I butted in and said, that I would prefer the library if it was possible. "I will see what I can arrange, but it will not be immediately," he said. It would be possibly two months before he could place me. I agreed, he was obviously agreeing to anything to keep me quiet so I took advantage. The library wasn't very big, but I could sit and read for the two hours three times a week.

He offered his hand to me and said, "I know you are not our normal type of person in here, but just see it through." I turned without shaking his hand or looking him in the eye.

I was shaking with anger, but also a part of me had something to look forward to. I could work in the library. This was the first chink of light in this otherwise dismal world of stone and men.

I thought afterward that the director probably breathed a sigh of relief as I walked out the door. I suppose I could have made it very difficult for him, I could have reported the incidents to the Maitre and demanded an enquiry, it is still a criminal offense to have your life threatened even in prison but I let him off lightly as I just latched onto the offer of something to fill the days. I got sent straight back to the cell to find Bento gone, but a slip of paper under the door.

The paper said I had a French lesson Thursday at 11:00 a.m.

I strolled back and forth in the cell, finishing off my interrupted promenade exercises until Bento arrived ten minutes later from promenade looking very despondent and repeating his usual "*putain*" over and over in a sentence I couldn't understand. I found out later that Elvis, Sheref, and Yannick had a "word" with him while on promenade. Did it stop him, though? What do you think? After all, he is a crackhead *dementi*.

My small order had arrived, too. A box of Lipton tea bags had never before and has never since looked so good. I could actually have a cup of tea, the first one since getting there. I made myself my first tea using the last butter I had left. I would ask the servers for a few extra at dinner, I thought, maybe offering a cigarette. I could now pay my tobacco/cigarette bill to Philip, too.

Bento just spent all day mumbling "put"*(poot)* this and "*put*" that. I didn't offer to make him a tea, but made a point of enjoying mine. He did eye up the cigarettes, though, knowing that I don't smoke. But he didn't say anything, apart from "*putain*" anyway.

CHAPTER TWELVE

The Reports

The afternoon came with a second treat, a second "promenade" out in the sunshine. We found out that the reason for this was so that the guards could "ring check" all the cell-window bars to make sure they all rang like a bell when hit, showing they hadn't been cut. What the heck? It was sunny and warm, and what more was there to do? Today, chasing the pigeons around the compound was a good feeling. Bento didn't walk around much, just stood in the corner talking to his fellow drug cronies. They didn't much like him either – the same as most people in here, they just tolerated him for "business."

I haven't said much about how I felt about the appeal-refusal letter, but writing this brings back the thoughts of how I thought in prison. I blocked it out most of the time, but while out in the compound on this unscheduled promenade, my only bit of freedom, it hit me hard this day. I had a knot in my stomach and throat. I kept trying to dismiss the feeling, but it wasn't going. It might have had something to do with the psychology of those "ringing bars." It just emphasised how impregnable it was in here, not just physically, but mentally too. It sounds silly now, but thoughts of escape entered my mind. I am sure I could get out. I looked up and around the compound, getting my bearings of where I was in the prison itself and in Limoges. I even asked Sheref about how easy it would be to get from France to Spain, and where to cross the border.

With a bit of thought, I knew I could do it. I even remember the rooflines in the hospital I stayed in for the day after the attack. Then the notion was dropped as the guard clattered the keys. It was time to go in. It stuck in my mind, though, not as something serious, but as a sign of desperation. I learned a lot of things about people being in here, and remembered things I had read over the years about prison, breakouts, and desperation. Now I understood why that thought of escape was so all-consuming. It was simply a release, a pressure regulator, a dump valve that, once in a while, desperation triggered. Some let it fester, and some just let it do its job and then let it go.

I just did the latter. The valve had done its job, and I just let it go with an internal grin that I could be so stupid.

As I walked through the gate, a *servient*, actually one of the nicer ones, pulled me to one side. As he frisked me, he said, "Your *avocat* is here, Prof. I will take you there."

There were a couple of nice guards in here, generally showing understanding or compassion to a fellow man in a difficult position. But in my short time here so far, I had become acquainted with one or two who were genuinely interested in you as a human being and not just a surname and number. This one walking me to see my *avocat* was Jean-Gerard, who stayed with me most of the day in the hospital ward. He was a fellow Citroen DS fan. Some of the guards had taken to calling me "Prof," obviously having acquired some knowledge as to my qualifications, but also recognizing that I was not their normal subject type. This didn't help much with the other inmate's view of me, and I think, to some extent – although I never really found out the truth – this was the reason behind my two attacks. Inmates like you to fit into a certain category, usually close to their own way, or they didn't trust you. And, although I had gotten quite good at explaining enough of the "computer fraud" reason I was in here, there was some obvious dissent.

Anyway, we arrived at the "*avocats*' interview room." I was told very early on that this was a free room inasmuch as, although there was a division, items pertaining to one's case were allowed to be passed. And I had heard that, sometimes, some *avocats* would supply drugs at this time, too, to those who required them or paid for the service. There was no guard, camera, or microphone here and, apart from the frisk going in, there was a very loose frisk coming out. As long as you declared that the envelope you were holding contained only case papers, the guard couldn't even touch it.

To enter this interview room, one had to walk through one set of doors into an "anteroom." The door behind you locked, then the second door buzzed to let you into the interview room.

On this occasion, I was met by a very sheepish and rather disheveled-looking Maître M. His office is just across the car park and bus station. He had obviously run all the way here.

I had planned a few times what I would say to him, including, "You're sacked, you waste of space." I managed to get out, "What happened, Maitre M?" before I just broke down in tears and slumped into my seat. "I am sorry" he replied. "I did all I could do, but "she" (the judge de detention) was adamant," he said. "She wants the psychological reports before she even considers releasing you. I have organized them already, and they may take a week or so to get round to you, but know you are a priority." For the next ten minutes, we just discussed how I was bearing up. He also mentioned that he had spoken to Trudy, but also that he had to tell her that he wasn't really allowed to and had to explain the reasons why.

He went on to say, "She did, however, say to pass on that she loves you and would see you soon." At the time, I didn't know whether that made my emotional state better or worse. I bid Maitre M farewell, thinking maybe he was actually doing all he could. I pushed the buzzer, and Jean-Gerard came to the door to let me out. He put his hand on my arm to silently ask if I was okay. He said to me, "It is very hard for you, I know. But I have faith in the system. They will see, Prof. They will see." That made me even more emotional, that even this man could see that I was innocent. Why couldn't the judge?

Wednesday came, and I stayed in the cell as Bento went out on promenade. I had the habit of pacing the room back and forth when on my own, but this was broken by a key rattle. The guard shouted, "Greene, *avocat*." This surprised me, as I wasn't expecting him back for any reason, especially so soon after visiting me already. I followed the guard to the visiting rooms and was surprised to see a woman I didn't recognize smiling at me. She held out her hand and introduced herself as Dominique O. She was lovely, attractive but not stunning. It was her radiant smile covering her whole face that made her so appealing. She looked very French, small and slim with slightly olive skin, dark, curly hair, and hazel-brown eyes

"I am from the British Embassy in Bordeaux, and have been requested to visit you to see if you are okay and that you are being treated well," she said.

At this point, I just broke down again. I apologized after I got myself together. But she said, "I am here just for you. I can listen to you, and I can try to help, although in a limited way."

She felt like a friend – someone I could talk to in English, someone to listen to me. I can remember a bit of what I said, but I just talked for what must have been an hour or so. She said she would come and visit me again, but was only allowed two visits before conviction. I passed on a couple of messages to pass to Trudy, and found out later that Dominique was quite a help for Trudy, telling her about the process and even insisting that Maitre M was the right man for the job. She contacted Prisoners Abroad, and they sent me stamps and envelopes as well as a monthly magazine. I could also send any "personal" letters to them, and they would pass them on to Trudy without them being scrutinized by the prison first. This was handy if I wanted to talk in any detail about the situation.

I left my meeting with Dominique feeling that I had a friend, as silly as that sounds. I had managed to unload in my own language, and she promised to help. I could write to her anytime, and she could write back. I did write her that very afternoon to thank her and to tell her how much her visit meant to me.

This Wednesday ended with the usual slop for dinner, then two episodes of *Prison Break Series 2*.

Thursday arrived. At 9:45 a.m., promenade was cold and fresh, but a little more bearable with the clothes Trudy had brought in for me, including a black fleece. When I got back to the cell, 11:00 a.m. arrived with a rattle of keys and "Greene, *ecole*" (school, French lesson) was shouted. Off I trotted, following the guard to places I had never ventured before. I remember thinking what a mess the prison was. The concrete floor looked like it had been hammered up, but this was just due to wear over the years.

On the way, we collected about a half dozen men and were led into a room that looked like a school classroom. My French lesson lasted about an hour and a half. I found out that I wasn't too bad at speaking French compared with my classmates, including a fifty-year-old Russian who not only couldn't speak French, but couldn't read or write either. Class was a break from the monotony of cell time, and I got back to the cell just in time for lunch.

I put my newly acquired writing books and pencil in my locker and noticed that my stuff had been gone through again. A razor and a bar of soap were gone, as well as a pack of cigarettes. I saw red this time. Without a word, I dragged Bento off the top bunk, where he was sleeping or pretending to be asleep. He just stopped himself from falling onto the floor. In one movement, I spun him around. Putting one arm around his neck, I pulled the toilet door open with my other arm, then stuffed his head down the toilet and flushed. As I turned, I kicked him in the ass so hard that he must have nearly gone around the toilet bend. He must have been in one of his drug-induced stupors, because he hardly reacted. He managed to get himself out of his precarious position, but said nothing and just accepted his fate. I looked him straight in his scared eyes, trying not to smile at the drips falling from his hair, and said, "I want them back, *now!*" He reached under his pillow and produced what he had taken. I couldn't think of anything to say at this point, and just pointed straight at his face. He got the point this time around! Nothing more this day was said. He just stayed in bed until teatime at 5:30

p.m., then he had his tea and went back to bed. As far as I could tell, this tactic worked for the rest of the time, as I used to arrange my possessions so I could tell if they had been moved, and they never had again.

Over the next few days, I had "collateral." I managed to buy more butter for my water boiler, so I was able to make a couple of cups of tea a day, making sure I wasn't caught by the guards. Although, saying that, I had a couple of near-misses. I also think they just turned a blind eye.

The "kettle-heated water from next door" method would work for days on end. Then along would come a "difficult" guard, and I would have to resort to an extra couple of cups from the fruit-tray boiler.

The morning two cups would be shared with Bento. He never once said thank you, but would always behave a bit more genially for at least ten minutes after. I think the cocaine must have zapped his long-term memory, as he would resort to his normal, obnoxious self shortly after nine minutes and fifty-five seconds.

I remember he got touchy about me changing the TV channel once when he wasn't watching it. He jumped down from his top bunk turned the channel back. He then turned the sound right up, but in doing so, he knocked his cup off the side and it smashed on the floor. He spent the next two hours shouting for the *servient* and kicking the door to get another one, as he would miss his morning cup from his neighbor. It made me smile. It took two days of him complaining before they got him another cup, and both mornings he would have a fit because he didn't get his tea. It seems so petty now, even the "head down the toilet" incident, but we had nothing else but our own possessions. Cups or butter, it was all we had.

I think it was toward the end of my third week that the keys rattled in the door at about 2:00 p.m. with the shout of "Greene, *avocat.*" It surprised me, as I hadn't expected Maitre M to visit, especially after his last conversation. My heart jumped in anticipation, but sunk just as quickly when I went through the doors to find a weaselly looking man sitting in the chair with a woman standing behind him, waiting for the guard to bring a second chair.

The woman spoke first, surprisingly in English with a soft, French accent. She said this is Mr. "something forgettable." He was a psychologist, she said, and was here for my assessment, as ordered by the judge. She said her name was Evelyn S, and I shook their hands. The weaselly man had a weaselly handshake, too. "What does one make of that?" I thought as one psychologist to another.

I took an immediate liking to Evelyn S. She was quite a short lady with messy hair, glasses, and a rather dowdy dress sense. I think her wardrobe choices were more functional than normal. At first, I thought she had rather a stern way about her, because she had rather an expressionless face. But I soon got used to her way. She looked as though she had been running.

Considering what I know of her now, she probably had been running. She works very hard, flitting about here and there between teaching in a college and appointments such as this. Due to tight schedules, she is usually late for one appointment or another.

On this day, she worked very hard to express what I was trying to get across to the psychologist, who, as you can imagine, was being very deep and needed a good translator.

I sat there for nearly two hours answering silly, formatted questions about my parents, my family, my children, and my relationships with all of the above. Most of the questions had disappeared from the psychologist vocabulary when Sigmund Freud died. I got slightly emotional at one point, but more out of anger than any other emotion. I was annoyed that I had to answer questions of a personal and at times explicit nature.

Madame Evelyn was great, and I could tell she was stressing the emotion and thoughts behind my words – something that would be very difficult under any circumstance, let alone in a prison in front of a suspected paedophile. The interview ended, and the psychologist explained that he would send the report in a week. As they left, I heard him say to Madame Evelyn while waiting to be released, "That man is not an abuser." I allowed myself to smile a little, inside though. I still had a psychiatrist to see.

On leaving the interview, I was met by Jean-Gerard, who asked the right sort of questions. "Things are moving, professor," he said. I smiled, not allowing myself to believe him and end up in a pit of despair again.

The very next day, the psychiatrist turned up, again with Madame Evelyn, and asked similar questions, but also included my medical history. He asked, "Any dementia in your family?" and that sort of rubbish. Have these so-called professionals not read recent papers on new techniques of questioning? When he asked me what I like to read, I said, "*The Dao De Jing* by Lao Tse and Jung." He quickly scribbled something on his pad instead of drawing lines of cohesion. If he thought I was taking the piss, he didn't show it. I wasn't, of course, as I do like to read it, but it sparked his interest.

This time, on exit of the room, I was met by Mr. Nasty. He didn't like me at all, and didn't try to hide it. He just sneered and escorted me back to my cell. As I bent down to enter the cell, he said something very quietly, so quietly I didn't catch it. And, by the time I turned and asked him to repeat it, he was closing the door. I only wondered for a minute what he had said, but it passed.

I think I probably came close to finding out about two days later. Keys rattled, and he appeared at the door saying, "Greene education," meaning French lesson. But I didn't have one booked. I didn't protest, and I followed, thinking maybe they had forgotten the slip under the door or that maybe Bento had picked it up. Halfway around the prison, in an area that I didn't recognize, I was told to stop. The guard went through a door, and out came two rough-looking black men I didn't recognize. At first, I just thought they were new French-class members, until they started to square up to me and poke me. They had very odd French accents, and I took them for Ghanaians. It took me a couple of seconds to realize what was going on, but I clicked when I heard the word "pedo" used. Only a very few guards knew why I was actually in here, and the guard that had escorted me to my French lesson was one of them. I was in trouble. He had always sneered at me, and now I was on a balcony trapped by two men who were up to no good.

The only way I can explain the position to you is like this. In every prison film, you see a gridded balcony looking down onto the floor below. This was the same. It was quite a secluded area, too, as it was above the solitary-confinement cells where I had spent my first few days. But it was also undergoing work.

I started to run for the swinging door I had come through to get to this balcony. Only to find it had locked itself from the outside. I had no option but to turn and run straight for the two men. One thing I was good at in rugby was a "hand down" to someone running at you. I did this to the first one, but the second was behind him and caught me square in the chest with his head before he went down. My heart pounded inside my rib cage as it felt the crash. I went down with a thump as one of them had hold of my leg. I was pushed by my chin under the lower walkway barrier. The pain in my head was so severe that I can still feel it now if I touch the same area. I did manage to roll and get out of that position, but soon wished I hadn't, as the guy who had hit me in the chest managed to get me over a fire bucket that was full of sand, ash, and cigarette butts. He pushed my head into it with his foot, and I thought I would suffocate in sand. What a horrible sensation that was. The smell of old and wet cigarette butts brings that memory back very often. It still makes me gag and shake even now, two years later.

Somehow, they managed to get me up on my feet while I was still choking from the sand. They had hold of my arms and started to push me over the balcony. If I hadn't just let them do it, I think I would have broken my back on the handrail. The pressure was intense. I went over the balcony backward and head first. My first thought was of the floor below, but a split second later, I landed in the wire-mesh netting that was there to protect people below from falling debris thrown by disgruntled inmates. This ended the ordeal, as the second I hit the netting, the alarms sounded – another security measure against people trying to jump from the balcony. Guards arrived to find me trying to roll over and get my bearings on what felt like a net trampoline.

One of the guards to arrive was Jean-Gerard, who was looking very concerned as, at first glance, it looked like I had jumped. They soon realized this was not the case when they caught a glimpse of the two black men running down the corridor. They were never identified, mainly because the guard who had escorted me had locked them back in their cells.

I was kicking and screaming, this time in English, out of shock more than anything. I wanted to see the director, then the service social woman, then the police. I didn't know what I was yelling at, but I actually just couldn't stop myself. It must have looked very bizarre, me lying face down in this mesh, shouting and screaming at anyone looking at me.

As the mesh extends to all the edges and is clipped into place, there is no way out other than the way you got there. One of the guards rolled out a steel rope ladder from the balcony for me to climb back up. I was shaking so much that it took me a while to get my balance and get onto the ladder. Even as I was climbing, I was shouting that I wanted the *gendarmes* in here now and that I wanted to bring charges. I knew the guard who allowed this to happen, and might have even orchestrated it.

I should have known better. I was just allowed to rest in the hospital wing again and was told it would be dealt with. I never saw the guard again on my side of the prison, but I know he was still around, as I saw him walk into the holding cell while I was walking to promenade one day.

None of these things happened officially. But for me, I still dream day and night of being thrown off that balcony. I still dream of suffocating in sand and cigarette butts. I still have day and night terrors of being strung up by my neck with a sheet. And I am sure I always will, for the rest of my life, with the right memory triggers. But none of it officially happened because French remand prisons are too full, too badly funded, and too understaffed. After all, I was just a lowlife not worth a bean.

I think it was the great Winston Churchill who said, "You can measure the civilization of a society by the way it treats its prisoners."

It is at this point that I leave the monotony of prison to your own meandering thoughts, as nothing of any great consequence happened to me after these incidents. But I have to mention, of course, that I did, however, start receiving communications from the outside world. About the fourth week in, I started receiving letters from people. My first one was from Sonia F, and it surprised the hell out of me. Firstly, I wasn't expecting to receive anything from anyone. But secondly, I wasn't expecting a letter from Sonia wishing me well and telling me to be strong. I was speechless. Then there was one from Sue W, and another from my friend John MR, who had sent me some yellow paper to calm my spirits. I also saw him many times in my times of meditation and quiet sleep. He is a man of immense energy, and I would say one of my saviors in that place. Then came letters from Richard and Nina H and others. It took a few days before a letter came from Trudy and Tyler. I was overwhelmed *every* time I received one, not only that people had taken the trouble, but that so many people were rallying around to support me. Up until now, I just expected everyone to have deserted me. The only communications I had received were the photos from Trudy in my clothes bag. Even so, I was still half expecting a letter from her saying she never wanted to see me again. I didn't know that everyone I knew had come out in my support. In fact, Nina's letter sounded like she was going to chain herself to the front of the building with a banner reading, "NG is innocent, FREE NG." It kept me going in the last weeks of my incarceration. Although I have gone to each individual personally and expressed my sincere thanks, I don't think those concerned will ever know how much those words on paper meant – probably because they did it without thought, out of love and concern for another human being, much like Sheref and Jean Gerard.

I hasten to add that my letter receiving pissed Bento off, which was a treat. He started calling me "*Monsieur le president!*" He never got one letter from anyone, apart from his *avocat*.

As I said before, other minor things happened in that prison, especially with the likes of Bento the crackhead in one's cell. But nothing more of any interest to you as a reader took place., I had my good days and my bad days. These days of despair will stay with me for a very long time, I think. I have had panic attacks regularly since, one in a supermarket not so long ago because I saw "*gesiers*" (gizzards) in the freezer section. The poor, humble pigeon is on my dislike list because every time I see one I think of the compound. I still see the little section of road that I could just make out from the top of my cell window. And every time I park in that car park in front of the prison, I go cold and feel myself walking quicker, trying to leave it behind me.

I have met up with Sheref a couple of times. He came to my house, but it is a very odd feeling having him there. I owe him a lot, really. I owe him my friendship, at least. But, in some way, seeing him brings the memories of walking the compound back to me. Although these memories were of the more pleasant side of the time I spent there, they were also some of my darkest moments mentally. Walking around in the open air was great, but the wanting to run into and through the walls to freedom and keep running was hard to bear.

I had never been scared of anything – and I mean anything. But, for the first time in my life, I felt fear, real fear. Even to this day, I have a problem with enclosed spaces. An elevator gives me a pounding heart, as it is four walls closing in on me. In small rooms like waiting rooms, I have to get up and walk around, or even just open the door and look out because I can. I only spent six weeks in that place, but it felt like sixty years, and I have come out an old man in my head. I cannot explain this feeling or sensation, and I don't really think I ever will.

CHAPTER THIRTEEN
"Greene Liberté"

The day started like any other. Shower, promenade, lunch, then I got ready for my 2:15 p.m. French lesson. The keys rattled in the door the same way they always did at about 2:10 p.m. I picked up my books and pencils, ready to meet the words "Greene education," but I heard "Greene *avocat*," then "leave them here" (meaning books, etc.). The normal stern face from this particular guard betrayed nothing of what was to come. I walked along the balcony and turned to walk down the steps. As I neared the bottom, there were two other guards smiling up at me. I sort of heard one of the say "prof" and *liberté*," but it didn't connect. I walked into the holding area and through the second set of doors after the normal frisk search, and there was Maitre M, smiling. "Do you know already?" he asked.

"Know what?" I asked naively.

The next words sounded like I was in water, the sound you hear when your head is under water in a swimming pool or bath and people are talking around you. "You are free to go."

"The judge has released you today," Maitre M continued. "There are a few conditions, and you will have to sign a few papers, but you are free to go." I felt tears welling in my eyes, but I held back a sob. "I must go to another appointment, but call me after the weekend," he said. He shook my hand firmly and said, "I told you I would do it." I think he was proud of himself that day, especially after I found out the reason why the judge had released me. I'll explain that later.

As I came out, Jean-Gerard and another guard were there to officially frisk me and escort me back to the cell, but I could see that they were overjoyed. If you slow a film down so the voices sound garbled and deep, that is how I felt at this moment, and it didn't leave me. I was escorted back to the cell and told, "You have five minutes to pack your things." The door was locked on me for the last time. I didn't say anything to Bento, as he was watching TV. But I started packing my things, and he looked inquisitively at me. "I am free to go," I said. He just stared at me and said one of his expletives. I think it was "putain prison."

The guard arrived back at the cell, and I walked out, following him without even a grunt from Bento. But I heard him kick the door from inside for the very last time. Jean-Gerard was over the moon. I could see it in his face, and even his eyes were glassy. He took me into the holding area through three doors and left me. As he turned away, he squeezed my arm and said, "*Bon courage*, prof" (Good luck, prof), and walked out. I turned and looked through a few sections of bars back into the prison. I saw him turn again to see if I was looking. He stuck his thumb up, and I smiled in a dazed sort of way.

I was kept waiting for what seemed ages, but was probably ten minutes. I was then led back through the doors I originally entered through six weeks ago and into the office. There was lots of paperwork to sign. The money

I had left was about one hundred and thirty euro, so I got that back. The guard said, "What do you want done with the *bon command*? That was the goods I had ordered, which amounted to a packet of green tea and two packs of cigarettes. "Give them to my neighbors," I said. That would be a nice surprise for their kindness with the kettle.

I was processed and led through the first electronic main gate into an anteroom between gates. The guard looked at the papers quickly and opened the gate. I walked through and found myself on the pavement facing the car park with a large black sack of clothes in my hands. The door shut with a clang behind me.

The feeling of the breeze on my face with no wall in front of me was awe-inspiring. But now I was lost, truly lost. I knew where I was, but my feet wouldn't work. I stood waiting to cross the road for a good five minutes, the prison entrance door to my back. There is a camera just above the door, and I turned and looked at it, wondering whether anyone was looking. I eventually walked across the road through the car park to the road and traffic lights I could see out my window. Why I did this, I don't know. I think I was getting my bearings. I walked back to the prison wall. I then crossed over again so I wasn't on the same side as the prison.

Then I realized – no one knows I am here. No one knows I am out. I have to tell someone. I saw a telephone booth over in the corner of the car park, so I wandered over, only to discover that it was a card-only box. I had to repeat to myself, "Get a grip; find a way home." I started walking, in a daze but walking. I knew if I walked in the direction of the court building, I would be able to get a taxi. I remembered that I had money. Yes, that's what I would do – I had more than enough to get a taxi.

I walked for about fifteen minutes, still not really getting to grips that I was outside. I felt like I was walking in sand. I just hadn't walked this far in a straight line for six weeks. I knew where I was, as I have taken the same route by car a thousand times. It just felt different.

I came across an estate agency called "Orpi." I looked in the doorway at the girl who sat at the desk. She must have thought I looked lost, as she came out to ask if there was anything she could do. I told her I needed a taxi but didn't have a telephone to call one. She joyfully said she would call it for me, and asked where I needed to go. I told her, and she passed it on. "Taxi will be five minutes. You can wait here," she said.

It turned up as she had said, and I was on my way. I had to go to my friends' house, as Naomi was still at home, and I wasn't allowed within fifty meters of her. My friends the Holdsworths had agreed to "put me up" right at the beginning.

I felt I wanted to surprise everyone. Why, I don't know, after this ordeal. I asked the driver if I could borrow his phone to call my son. He happily agreed. I called his number. He answered the phone with a questioning "Hello?," as he didn't recognize the number, and all I could think of saying was, "Tyler, it's Dad."

"Oh my God," he said out loud. "You have been released, haven't you? You haven't just escaped?"

Tyler was on his way back from *lycée* in the coach, and as he cried out loud on the bus, I could hear his friends in the background shouting with joy that his dad had been released.

I explained to him what to do after he pulled himself together, and he called ahead to Denise and Gordon Holdsworth for me, then rang me back. He would share the news with Trudy when he got home, but he wanted to see me first, so would come straight to Denise and Gordon's house to meet me. He was as emotional and as excited as I was quickly becoming. The water was clearing from my ears and eyes.

I was on my way home – well, nearly anyway. But I was free and out in the open air, driving down a road I knew, seeing trees and houses I had seen before. But I wondered whether I would see them again. Freedom smelled good. No more of that constant, musty, damp smell of prison. No more of that constant noise of yelling and whistling. Most of all, no more keys jangling.

CHAPTER FOURTEEN
The Early Weeks After Release

Arriving at Gordon and Denise's was an emotional moment. I think I sobbed on Denise's shoulder for ten minutes, then she put the kettle on for a proper cup of tea.

An hour later, Gordon went off to pick Tyler up as, his bus had just arrived. He came straight to me at Gordon and Denise's, and it started again. We sobbed for about five minutes in each other's arms. Logistically speaking, he had made an excuse to Trudy, saying his bus was a little held up and would be about a half hour late. He eventually left, telling me he would see me in the morning, as he was going to stay at home to keep an eye on the other two while Trudy came to see me. Off he went. He hadn't told Trudy that I was free so that he could do it in person. I heard that Trudy collapsed on the floor outside the back door with emotion when he shared the good news. He told her away from prying eyes and ears. She came straight around to me via Gordon's car.

The arrival was incredibly emotional, as you could imagine. We held each other so tight, and it felt like we were standing outside in Gordon and Denise's garden for ages. Trudy was able to stay the night, as Tyler was looking after the other two children, but I had to get her back home by about 7:00 a.m. so Naomi wouldn't be aware she had been out all night.

That first night back was the worst, but there were other similar nights when I just couldn't stay in the room. I had to get up and just look out the window. I was terribly disoriented.

I was only in prison for about six weeks, so I can't imagine how it must feel to come home after years in a place like that.

I can remember just lying there in Trudy's arms all night. She felt thin, as she had lost so much weight. I didn't really sleep though the night, and as for the terrors, this worried Trudy greatly. I lashed out at the slightest movement.

At one point later on in the year, I actually thumped her. I hit her quite hard with my fists when she moved once while I must have been in a nightmare. That really upset me, and Trudy too. But she was very courageous and didn't say too much about it.

On the Saturday morning after dropping Trudy off at home (on the corner so I didn't go too close to the house), I went back to Gordon and Denise's house. I met Gordon, who was about to take the dog for a walk, so I joined him. Even that was a surreal feeling, after only having a compound and cell to pace. Walking in the forest on wet leaves was the oddest feeling.

Denise made breakfast, and I went to meet the boys to take them out to lunch.

The order from the judge said that I wasn't to leave the country, although I kept my passport. I had to sign at the *gendarmerie* every two weeks on a Monday morning. I was to have no contact with Naomi, but was allowed home as long as she wasn't there (i.e., when she was at school). I was required to stay at Gordon and Denise's house until such times as Naomi was no longer at home.

It was already set in motion to find Naomi alternate placement, as she was no longer welcome at home by any of the others. Even her brother was disgusted with her. But where David was concerned, he would just react the same way as everyone else.

The placement was confirmed just two days before Christmas, after having spent five weeks at Gordon and Denise's house. My stay with them had been very pleasant, and they had made me feel very welcome.

Opening your home to someone in this kind of situation takes a very special kind of person and, in Denise and Gordon, you have two very special people. It didn't stop there. For the next two years, they stayed with us every step of the way, taking Trudy to meetings at which I was not allowed to be present and not just coming to the judge with me nearly every time, but taking me so that I never had to think about driving.

In the five weeks before I went home, I could see Trudy every Friday and Saturday evening, when she would come and stay with me at Gordon and Denise's house. Occasionally, I had a bit of time at my own home during the day while Naomi was at school. Even my own home felt wrong. It didn't feel like it was mine anymore. I felt like a guest. I have never had an affair, but it felt a bit like I was doing something wrong, an illicit meeting of sorts.

I used to take the boys out on the weekends. That was fun, and it pissed Naomi off. She actually got jealous. She started writing bizarre letters to me, although she was never allowed to send them, of course. At one point, she made it clear that she wanted Trudy and Tyler out of the way so she could have me to herself. This was bizarre behavior for a so-called abused person. I feared she was becoming obsessed. It made me think of the Oedipus complex, also known as the Electra complex when it involves a female becoming obsessed with a parent of the opposite sex and wishing to destroy the other same-sex parent. It made me shiver, and the more I heard, the more I thought and still think there might have been a connection, but it wasn't pursued at the time.

Over the five weeks at Gordon and Denise's house, I learned a bit more about what was going on with Naomi. I know it sounds ridiculous, but I actually felt concerned for her. She was obviously sick and needed help. But I was helpless, too, because, according to the powers that be, I might have been the one who drove her to this. I couldn't really express how I felt to Trudy either, as she is a bit of a "what you see is what you get" sort of person, and only turned it around to give her an excuse to direct more anger at Naomi, especially as, as she reminds me often, I wasn't there to see the way she was when I was incarcerated or even at Gordon and Denise's house. Even now, this is a bit of a "bone of contention" with Trudy. I find it a bit like *the* conversation stoppers women have when pain is mentioned. "You men will never understand pain until you have had a baby." Enough said!

Anyway, back to the history On the December 23, Naomi was taken to what the French refer to as a "foyer," a girl's home, actually, and this allowed me to come home. We actually had a very rushed Christmas, as you could imagine. But at least I was at home to experience it, even if

I did feel like a startled rabbit caught in car headlights.

I have jumped ahead slightly, so I am going to step back to my first week of freedom, when Maitre M asked me for a rendezvous at his office. I waited about ten minutes for Maitre M to be ready for me, and I was eventually guided into his office. He passed the usual pleasantries and asked how I was feeling. After a short discussion about what he had done so far –I think to reassure me that he had been working hard on my behalf – he told me what had been the final clincher as to why I was released in a rush on that Friday before. Apart from my psych reports being absolutely fine and the authorities finding nothing untoward in my behavior, Maitre M had found a statement from the Naomi's psychiatrist stating that, "Considering all that she has allegedly been through, Naomi shows absolutely *no* 'familiar' behavior expected from an abused child." When Maitre M put that in front of the judge with all the other information gathered about me, she had no choice but to sign off on the release. This, at the time, made me happy – but also angry, because why the f#*k was I still being treated like a criminal?

With all this and the fact Naomi was still a virgin (intact), everything she had said was a lie. All Maitre M could do was to say, "The process has to be seen through. It will take up to two years to complete. You are in it for the long haul, but I am there with you every step of the way."

I left the office saddened that this wasn't over and that it would be a tough two years. But at least I left his office and wasn't still in that "godforsaken place" for the next two years – which, he assured me, I would have been if they had any reason to keep me there.

CHAPTER FIFTEEN

Under Judicial Control

The *juge d'instruction* is one of the most powerful people in France, and has been so since the revolution. He or she investigates all *crimes* (severe offenses like rape and murder) and may also be given a mandate to investigate lesser offenses if they are serious or complex. There is nothing to compare them with in the Anglo-Saxon justice system, in which the police investigate then have to convince a judge and sometimes a jury that the defendant is guilty.

The powers granted to this person are so vast that JIs have been described as the most powerful figures in the republic. The juge is expected to examine evidence both for and against the charges. He or she is basically a super sleuth armed with judicial impartiality. Whether or not JIs succeed in this endeavor is to be seen, but plans are afoot to review this role, especially after the case known as the "Outreau fiasco." In this case, the defense team was unable to convince the courts that the examining magistrate had gotten it wrong, and thirteen innocent people spent a total of more than two hundred and fifty years in prison after allegations of paedophilia. Since this case many lawyers and politicians have called for the position to be abolished. It was only after this case that a criminal-justice reform has been written into the lawbooks requiring that a person should be presumed innocent until found otherwise. Many defense lawyers, however, still feel that some judges' attitudes toward defendants mean they are required to prove their clients' innocence rather than be able to rely on the principle that the prosecution should prove their guilt. This often led to a large number of defendants finding themselves locked up while supposedly legally being presumed innocent on the decision of the very person supposedly impartial enough to investigate both sides of the case. It was therefore felt necessary to separate the investigation function from the power to imprison, hence the *"Juge de detention et liberte."* Not that this helped in my case, as the *juge de detention* didn't even give me a chance to explain anything, presumed my guilt, and spat it back at me.

Overall, the lawyers of France are starting to realize, albeit slowly, that their job has to change. They have to be more defensive in the defense of a client instead of just an arbitrator of the process. Even my own *avocat* came to realize this, thankfully, during my own incarceration and subsequent investigation.

One of the conditions of my release was to visit the *gendarmerie* every two weeks on a Monday, officially between 2:00 p.m. and 4:00 p.m. The first time I had to do this was about a week after my release, and it was at the *gendarmerie* at which this whole episode started. Walking up to the gate and pressing the buzzer was hard enough. But when the gate opened and I had to enter the same door and go into the same office, I froze. My legs just did not want to work. Gordon had come along with me for moral support, and God did I need him that day. I shook and my heart pounded in my throat as I walked up the steps and opened the pair of doors. The *gendarme* behind the counter smiled and offered his hand to shake. He was one of the nicer ones, I remember. It lightened my mood very slightly. He reached under the desk for a folder already prepared for my visit, pulled out a blank sheet of paper, drew a couple of lines on it, and asked that I sign and date it. I did this and left the building as quickly as I could, my mind racing at the thought of being kept behind.

Over the following two years of signings, the only hiccup was the fact that the local town *gendarmerie* was not always manned. The first time this happened was on Christmas Eve. I panicked, thinking that if I didn't sign between the times of 2:00 and 4:00 p.m., I would be rearrested and sent back to prison. So I demanded to change the signing to a town about ten kilometers away, as it was manned twenty-four hours a day and open to the public seven days a week from 8:00 a.m. From that day on, I signed there, and usually at 8:00 a.m. to get it over and done with. Although, on a couple of occasions, I had early appointments, so I couldn't, but just did it when I got back. Occasionally, I got a "nice" *gendarme*. Other times, I got an arrogant, sneering, whispering one. I held my head high *every time* I walked in and walked out again. And, although I didn't really feel like it inside, I tried to have an air of confidence about me. It worked, too, as you could occasionally see on their faces an air of confusion as I swanned in, signed, and swanned back out again, bidding them a good day.

The very last day I had to sign was a good one for me. I had the letter from the judge to say it was all over on a Saturday morning post, so come the Monday I was prepared to wave this in their faces with a triumphant smirk. But, as I walked through the door at 8:00 a.m. on the Monday after, there were three officers behind the counter, including one of the original officers who had been at the *gendarmerie* on the first day. The one I always called the nice one had a big smile on his face and said, "You don't need to be here. We have had the letter from the judge." I actually saw real happiness in his smile. I wondered if he had been secretly rooting for me too?

The request for "convocation" with the *juge d'instruction* always came in the form of two letters – one to be signed for, an "*avis de reception*," and, a day or so later, a normal letter. I would call or e-mail Maitre M to make sure he would be there. The first time this happened, obviously, was the most nerve-wracking, but Maitre M asked me in for a rendezvous with him to discuss how it was to proceed.

Basically, I would sit in front of the judge in her office. There would be a couple of others in the room, too, most likely a "junior" learning the job and a person to transcribe every detail. I would be allowed a translator at all times. I would be asked questions, and I was to answer them as clearly as possible. This was easier said than done through a translator, but I had to do it, as my life and liberty depended on it.

The first time was obviously the most memorable – bar one, but we will get to that later.

The JI, as I will call her again so as to not write the name every time, was her normal surly self, but I was pleased to again meet Evelyn, my translator. I spent three hours on that first interview answering the JI's questions, from the very basic family-oriented ones to more serious ones about family life at home and how this had affected everyone. I was very precise, detailed, and honest with my answers. I made it very clear how important it was that she should make contact with social services in the UK, as I was certain there was an answer to all of this there. I still don't know to this day whether she did, other than to get the report written by the children's psychologist translated.

She said to me at one point that it was not up to her to go traipsing around Europe looking for information. I, however, made it very clear (in a respectful manner) that it was indeed her duty to do so to get to the bottom of all of this. Otherwise, she would be putting an innocent man away.

Gordon and Denise *always* took us to every meeting to give us moral support. Trudy always came, too.

By the end of the convocations, I was always mentally exhausted at having to answer the same things over and over, requested to remember things that were just fleeting moments in family life as though my life depended on it. It seemed that I had to justify everything I had said and done as a father in this family, and was being treated as someone unusual because I would openly kiss and hug my children or sit and talk to them openly about sexual matters rather than lying or avoiding the subject.

She not only had a suspicious way of looking at me, but the way the questions were stressed indicated that she more often than not thought I was lying – not including, of course, when she actually, point blank told me she thought I was. Maitre M assured me that she was just doing it to get at the truth. I think personally that she had been watching too many "good cop, bad cop" movies. For one of the "most powerful women in the republic," I nearly always thought she seemed out of her depth.

As for Evelyn, I quickly learned that she was supporting

me, too, and verbally. Not only was she supposed to be very accurate, but also unbiased in her translations. But I started detecting empathy in her voice and in the wording of my answers. I found out later that she had been given the documents received from social services in the UK to translate for the court. In fact, she officially translated everything that came in to the court in English. She was getting a more in-depth view of the situation than anyone else. We managed to build up a good rapport with each other in our convocations with the JI, and I found out a lot about her own "adoption problems" and those of friends she knew in similar situations. To this day, I feel she had a big hand in my acquittal, purely via the words of mine she spoke and how she spoke them. I needn't have worried that I would not get over what I had to say.

Someone "up there," whomever that might be, was watching over me. I will forever be grateful to her. She put herself in a situation that could have gotten her in a lot of trouble. But, as she said to me the last time we met in court, it had to be done, otherwise something unbearable might have happened that she would not have wanted to be party to. She, too, recognized how flawed the system was in that *just one* person had that much power over a situation such as this.

I mentioned briefly the "other memorable" time with the JI, and that was the convocation with me and Naomi. I was warned of the occasion, but seeing her at the court building was not easy for me. I had lots of mixed emotions – a part of me wanted to walk up to her and hug her, and another part of me just wanted to shout at her, "*Why Naomi?* Why have you turned on me?" I also had to deal with the hate in Trudy's eyes and, while in the waiting area, kept a tight hold of her hand to keep her from launching at least verbal abuse at her, at worst physical harm.

Naomi was giving a good display of a cocky teenager, rocking on her chair with her arms folded and chewing gum. When the judge eventually got started, it was with Naomi. It was not to my glee but to my surprise that she fed Naomi her first lines and questions and just watched her as the lies started falling off her tongue. Apparently, Naomi was an angel and had never had boyfriends until the judge handed her statements from "friends" at school who thought otherwise.

She claimed that she had never engaged in or even talked about anything sexual, until the judge read aloud statements from "boys and teachers" at school. The extent to which her flirting behavior had reached included grabbing private parts and offering "blow jobs."

The judge then started the questioning about the situation. She asked Naomi if she had ever had sexual intercourse with me. She answered "yes." When the judge asked her to describe the place, it was totally different from that of her original statement. When asked why, she said she was "nervous and embarrassed."

Then the judge pulled out the police report that said Naomi was calm, confident, and clear about what had happened and how she explained it. She just rocked more on her chair and gave an indifferent stare, one that I knew too well from when she had lied to us about something. I wanted to jump up and shout, "Look at that face. She knows she is lying!" But I restrained myself – the judge was doing well enough.

"You were very clear on what your father was wearing on the day you said he raped you. Please describe it for me," said the JI. She couldn't.

JI: "What shape was the table?"

Naomi: "Square."

JI: "In the statement, you said it was round"

Naomi: "No, definitely square."

JI: "Was it a high table?"

Naomi: "No, low like a coffee table."

JI: "You said it was a dinner table."

Naomi: "I was confused." She just went red, and so did her *avocat*.

JI: "Social services in the UK said you were abused in the UK by your previous family. Is that true?"

Naomi: "No! They were okay, but always busy, so couldn't look after us."

JI: "So social services are telling lies?"

Naomi: "Maybe they confused me with someone else."

The JI then turned to me to confirm a few things and to ask how I felt about what Naomi had said. I just said that she had confirmed everything I had already said. For the first time, the judge looked at me differently. We spent another hour going over other questions, but all the time Naomi could not get her story straight.

I left that convocation a little bit lighter, and it must have showed, as Naomi just stood on the other end of the waiting area and stared and glared at me. What surprised me was her lack of acknowledgment that she had lied. She seemed oblivious to it. That's more than I can say for her *avocat*, though. She looked thoroughly pissed off!

The convocations carried on for almost eighteen months. They were usually held once, sometimes twice a month, and consisted of questions, answers, and another convocation in front of Naomi. Then, the judge declared on one occasion that this was the last convocation for her to collate all the information and make a decision. She could decide to dismiss without fault, find guilty and convict for sentence in front of the *juge de detention*, send the case to a procurator for further assistance, or send the case to trial in front of a court.

After another two months of waiting after this, I found out through pestering Maitre M that the decision had gone to the procurator for confirmation. I understand this to be a recent development in French law that a second person looks over the evidence, so as not to put the burden totally on one person – a step forward if only a small step.

Of all the times it could have arrived, it was when Trudy was visiting her parents in the UK that I received an e-mail with an attachment faxed from the court building with the decision. Maitre M just said congratulations, it is over. There was no case to answer.

I could have been found "not guilty" or "non culpable," which could mean "found not guilty" due to a lack of evidence or for other reasons. *But no* – I was completely vindicated with a non lieu, which meant "no case to answer."

I collapsed in a heap and sobbed. Eventually, I called Gordon. The phone call to Gordon was garbled, as I could not find the words to say, and he came straight around to see me. Denise must have beat the "tom-tom drums" so the word got around. Fearing I would not handle it on my own, I was inundated with visitors and three bottles of champagne.

As nice as it was, I now just wanted to be alone to call Trudy. I had to wait for everyone to go home. At about 10:00 p.m., I called. I didn't say a lot. I managed to get the words out, and then we sobbed together on the phone. She wanted to come home immediately, but I said no, it was fine. In the next few days, I pulled myself together and, for that moment, felt like I was walking on air. After two years of hell, it was over – apart from the fact that I didn't have the official discharge letter yet, and that took another two weeks to prepare and receive. Talk about slow.

CHAPTER SIXTEEN
Friend or Foe

Of all the friends who stood by me and supported me, there were as many who either dropped me like a hot potato, would hide whenever they came across me in a supermarket, or blatantly gossiped about me either behind my back or, sometimes, with shallow whispers in my earshot. I suffered stares, whispers, and point-blank name-calling.

Before this incident, I would always care about what people thought of me. But now, they didn't matter to me and, really, they do not even deserve a mention. The people who stuck around and put themselves out are the only ones that need a mention, not by name but by deed. Those individuals will probably be reading this, too, and you will know who you are. To these people, I thank you from the bottom of my heart:

- those who wrote to the judge in anger and protest that this could be happening;

- those who would ring me *everyday* to see if I was okay;

- those who would call me in the evening after a convocation to see if I was okay;

- those who gave me good luck messages before I went

to the convocation;

- those who remembered *every* other Monday "at the *gendarmerie*" and sent me a message of good luck;

- those who rallied around my wife and family while I was in that hellhole and after;

- those who drove many kilometers to see Corinne (the personality assessor for the court) and gave me a glowing reference;

- most important of all, my wife and my son, who were there every minute of every day without even a thought that I could be guilty, going through just as hard a time as me, but not showing it for my sake, putting on a brave face for me, and hurting twice – once for me and once for them.

Corinne, the personality assessor mentioned earlier, actually said that this was the first time in her career when *everyone* to whom she spoke gave honest, unforced compliments as to the sort of person I really was. She said that I was "much loved." Those words from a complete stranger will never leave me.

I said to Arnie, a very dear friend of mine, that one thing that worried me was that I would be different – closed, unloving, and selfish because I had been shit on one time too many. He agreed with me. "You will be different," he said, "but for the better. We are *only* here to learn, and one day you will have the opportunity not only to apply what you have learned, but to help someone else in a way previously unimaginable."

It doesn't help get rid of the nightmares, daymares, and memories, or even the thoughts of failure to some extent, but I cope with these things, holding my head higher than ever.

CHAPTER SEVENTEEN
Aftermaths for the Children

After I was released from judicial control and therefore allowed contact with Naomi again, I was invited to a couple of foyer meetings to discuss her progress through school and into work. We even had to go through a number of court hearings to stipulate that she stay exactly where she was. We were expected to resume motherly and fatherly control again, even to the point of having her back in the family. We refused this, saying that there is no way this would work physically. We would forever be treading on eggshells, wondering when the next revelation would bring the *gendarmes* to our door.

I still cannot get over the fact that I have failed her in some way. Trudy resents her to such an extent that she doesn't feel any emotion toward her other than hate – and this is understandable, as I understand the way my wife copes. As for me I don't and can't find it in my heart to hate anyone. The trouble with this is that it just leaves me broken-hearted for the umpteenth time. It breaks my heart thinking that, after all we have been through, Naomi will have to bear the brunt of this on her own. She will have to come to terms with what she did, not only to us individually or as a family, but to herself. The alternative, of course, is that she doesn't come to terms with anything and just goes on in her own sweet way, oblivious to the hurt she causes or leaves behind in her wake. I don't know which is worse, for me at least.

David, her brother, didn't fare too well, either. He suffered from many afflictions over the years, and there is no telling whether any of this really made him worse. But I feel all this prematurely pushed him over the edge. He ended up with schizophrenia, multiple personality disorders, and mild epilepsy, culminating in a long stay in a mental institute under strong drugs to keep him from being violent. He is, and will stay, in a support environment, probably for the rest of his life. We have contact, but most of the time we are forgotten. He lives in his own little world.

For Me

The aftermath, for me at least, is resorting to this – writing it all down to stay sane.

We ended up selling the house we loved and spent three years renovating not only because we could not get rid of the feeling that it no longer belonged to us but all the reasons we came to France had been taken away from us. Over the course of the investigation, everything Naomi and I had ever done together – working on the house or during our time together – had been destroyed. What I saw as me being not just a good father but a good Dad – spending quality time with all my kids – had been tainted by her adding some kind of sexual connotation. I grew too to loathe the place. It had, for me, all these visions and memories of the past four years emanating from the walls. The situation cost us dearly financially, too; in excess of 15,000 .

We sold it and moved on to find something for Trudy and me to start again, something that had never been touched by the hands of adopted, damaged children.

The people around us who took the "no smoke without fire" view, presuming me guilty even after being exonerated, in the end also contributed to driving us away. Holding one's head high only goes so far with one's own dignity. It doesn't make the days bearably happy when you step foot outside your own door and feel vilified by passing neighbors.

I haven't changed as a person, but I have changed inside. I feel that I am a sadder person and more hurt by this experience than by anything before, but what I feared about being different hasn't happened. I still cannot say no to people. I still want to be a human doing, not just a human being.

At time of this writing, we have moved to a lovely cottage, small and cozy just for us. I am renovating again, so my mind is on that most of the time. I still have panic attacks and memories of the terrifying experiences, and at times I feel as though I could just pack a bag of essentials and walk away from everything. *Yes – everything!* But, deep down, I know the experience would follow me, even in memories.

I plucked up the courage to have a blood test too; I didn't go to the doctors especially for this as I had an inner ear infection but while there I asked the doctor to do one and told him the circumstances of my fears. The results were back within a week of asking and were thankfully negative but this also allowed me to not have to say anything to anyone about the rape. It took 3 years before I managed to burst out the words to my wife and son.

For Trudy

As for Trudy, the experience has taken, I fear, an irreparable toll. The anxiety and torment of someone she loved has turned her own anxiety and torment into anger and hate. She has two new defence mechanisms – aggressiveness and acting dumb. The person I married was a vibrant, intelligent, thoughtful human being. Acting dumb just keeps her out of anything. If she doesn't know, there is nothing she can do about it. If that doesn't work, getting aggressive usually does the trick. All those feelings she felt during the investigation were like a drug. Now, she doesn't have that "high" – it has to be manifest in an alternative way. Some people go looking for another high. Others just say, "I don't want to do anything anymore, because it's easy keeping out of it." I have faith in her. I know she will eventually see the light, but under her own terms. Any amount of encouragement brings out the aggressor. Guess which one I will get for writing this. Trouble is, I love her like no other. She stuck by me, and I will stick by her.

For Tyler

Tyler lives in his own little world most of the time, much like his mother. In that way, he is just happy to be around his friends and family and sees things in black and white. But he is still someone I am so very proud of, proud to be near, and proud to have walk by my side. He is living proof I did something right not just as a father but as a Dad.

CHAPTER EIGHTEEN
Never Ending

I was busying myself in the garden last Sunday afternoon (in June 2010) and a gendarmerie van appeared at the gate. As always, my heart sank and my hands began to shake. Two rather short, stocky *gendarmes* dressed in their normal blues and looking very official and stern waited for me to walk to the gate, which I tried to do with the confidence of an innocent man, but didn't really succeed at. Sharply, I was told by the younger of the two that I had convocation with the "*chef du brigade*" (chief of the station) and was expected immediately at the *gendarmerie*. It all came flooding back in that instant.

Tyler drove me there and, whereas I often complain about the speed he drives, he seemed as though he was dawdling. "Get a move on," I said. I wanted this over and done with.

The building itself was set back off the road with a large, external spiral staircase to the first floor, but also to the front desk. I took the steps two at a time, leaving Trudy and Tyler behind. Bursting through the door in a fake air of confidence, I was met by a six-foot-six-inch, ex-rugby-playing *gendarme*. He put his hands in the air, telling me to be calm. He said, "*Vous étes le victime*" (You are the victim). He had a kindly face, despite his size, and revealing an air of sympathy, he removed a dossier from his desk.

It transpires that the same couple who had made our lives hell in our previous village had decided once again to make their presence felt. They had said to another person some time ago that they would not leave us alone. Wherever we moved in France, they would find us – and that was exactly what they had done. This was backed up by a letter – unsigned, undated, and unaddressed – sent to all our neighbors stating that I was a dangerous pervert and that I should be watched closely. Fortunately, none took it seriously, but someone contacted the gendarmerie. I spent the next two hours making a statement, but most of what I was saying had already been checked and added to the dossiers from the previous instances. This time, for the first time, the couple's action was taken seriously. Charges are mounting and will move forward as long as they can prove it was them with fingerprints, DNA, and postal references.

My neighbours are being very supportive to the point of waving vigorously and tooting the horns of their cars as they drive past but haven't mentioned it while talking.

Where I go from here I don't know

There is a continuation of the story where Naomi is concerned, too. While in the UK a couple of months ago, I started receiving text messages just saying "Hello!" I knew instantly who it was, but just let her continue. When eventually I did answer her, I made it clear in no uncertain words that I was keeping a copy of everything she wrote and that, the second she got abusive, that would be it. I would change my phone. I continue to talk with her by text, and I write her letters, too.

I cannot let her back into my life, but I wish her no harm and all the best for the future, for her future. I have never raised the subject of her allegations, and neither has she. But, as always, it goes full circle. I have had a few questions answered, even though I haven't asked a question. That, for me, is a kind of closure on at least a couple of items. It's probably the only closure I will ever get.

≥≥≥≤≤≤

Lightning Source UK Ltd.
Milton Keynes UK
UKHW01f0637050618
323753UK00001B/108/P